Brief Lives:
Anton Chekhov

Brief Lives:
Anton Chekhov

Patrick Miles

ET REMOTISSIMA PROPE

Brief Lives
Published by Hesperus Press Limited
4 Rickett Street, London sw6 1ru
www.hesperuspress.com

First published by Hesperus Press Limited, 2008

Designed and typeset by Fraser Muggeridge studio
Printed in Jordan by Jordan National Press

ISBN: 1-84391-900-1
ISBN13: 978-1-84391-900-1

Contents

I will truthfully, that is artistically, describe to you life, and you will see in it what you haven't seen before, haven't noticed: its contradictions, how it deviates from the norm…

Chekhov

Childhood: Freedom and Claustrophobia
1860–75

Sneezes and other bodily reflexes play a vital part in Chekhov's comic stories, so it seems appropriate that the surname Chekhov means approximately Sneasley. For hundreds of years Russian peasants nicknamed a child that sneezed at birth 'Chokh' ('Sneeze'), and his progeny became Chokhovs (Sneezleys). One of Anton Chekhov's uncles still called himself Chokhov. Anton's upwardly mobile grandfather, father and other uncle adopted the more genteel 'e'.

But there was no denying the Chekhovs' lowly origins. Anton's grandfather, Egor Chekhov, was born a serf of Count Chertkov in Voronezh Province, and his father Pavel was also a serf until the age of sixteen. In 1841 the ruthless, hard working and eccentric Egor bought himself and his family out of slavery and headed south to the steppes around Taganrog on the Azov Sea, where he became an estate manager.

One cannot exaggerate the influence of the steppe on Anton Chekhov's love of personal and spiritual freedom. In the first nineteen years of his life he spent many summer months on his grandfather's and friends' homesteads in the Don Steppe, he came to know 'every gully' as he said later, as well as the ancient burial mounds, the tumbleweed, the birds of prey, the vast starlit nights, the windmills, the peasant children and the Jewish innkeepers – all the elements of his masterpiece 'The Steppe' (1888). Free to wander, observe and interact, he had at least one epiphanic experience, as recounted by his brother Mikhail:

> Once, when he was still a schoolboy... somewhere in the steppe, Anton Pavlovich was standing by a deserted well, looking down at his reflection in the water, when a girl of about fifteen came up to draw water, and so charmed the future writer that there, in the steppe, he began to embrace her and kiss her, and then they stood together at the well a long time, in silence, staring down at their two reflections. He did not want to leave her, and she had forgotten all about her water. He told Suvorin this once, when they were talking about lives being like parallel lines, whether they can ever meet, and love at first sight.

The incident prefigures a major theme in Chekhov's writing: communication between people ('selves') and its relation to what he usually called 'the sexual sphere'.

If the steppe was where you were free, the town of Taganrog epitomised the opposite. Chekhov was born there, in a tiny one-storey house, on 16th January 1860, although his birth certificate says 17th January probably because that is his 'nameday' (St Antony the Great in the church calendar). Pavel Chekhov had married Evgeniia Morozova, ten years his junior, in 1854, and Anton was the third of their seven children. Since his father's name was Pavel, Anton's middle name became Pavlovich. As part of his scheme for self-advancement, Pavel nominated Greeks as Anton's godparents. Although basically a shopkeeper dealing in general stores, he had bought himself into the 'Second Guild of Merchants', a rung on one of the many hierarchies riddling Russian life. The Black Sea Greeks who had settled in Taganrog were some of its most successful businessmen. Their new houses have been described as looking like safes. Money, in Taganrog, was everyone's obsession.

The Chekhovs had very little of it. In the first four years of Chekhov's life they moved house three times, sometimes living with relations. Much of Pavel Chekhov's apparently improving prosperity was founded on credit raised by his networking. He was not a natural salesman. He short-weighed, short-changed, and sold stale food. He was more interested in pontificating to his regulars, who treated the shop as a club, and in his status as choirmaster at the cathedral and police alderman.

Within the family, Pavel Chekhov was a despot whose usual response to a difficulty was verbal abuse and physical violence. He stormed at his submissive wife and beat his sons unmercifully. Chekhov never forgave him this and his elder brothers were traumatised by it. In addition to making them work all hours in his shops, Pavel dragooned Aleksandr, Nikolai and Anton into singing at three services every Sunday and rehearsing long evenings. Taganrog's congregations were admiring of the results, but in Anton's words the boys 'felt like little convicts'. The association of church with coercion put him off organised religion for life.

At the age of seven Chekhov was sent to a Greek primary school. His father's idea was that with fluent Greek he could become a broker in a Greek trading house, or even attend Athens University. By the end of the year, however, Anton and Nikolai had barely mastered the Greek alphabet, so they were enrolled in the preparatory class of Taganrog Grammar School.

In many ways this institution was a microcosm of the Russian state: uniform and rank were all-important, literature and the sciences were marginalised as dangerous, a permanent inspector could enter boys' homes to root out 'subversion', and the teachers took bribes. The figures of the 'Man in a Case' (1898) and Kulygin in *Three Sisters* (1901) probably draw on Chekhov's experience there. Nevertheless, corporal punishment was forbidden and academic standards high. The rival claims of church and shop, together with the increasing chaos of family life as the Chekhovs packed their house with lodgers, meant that Anton made slow progress. By the age of fifteen he had stayed down two years because of poor performance in Maths, Geography and Greek. His forcible immersion in liturgy and the Bible, however, had a useful side-effect: Religious Knowledge was one of his best subjects, together with German.

Chekhov was motivated in his German by a Dr Schrempf, who had treated him for life-threatening peritonitis contracted from swimming in a cold river on a visit to the steppe in 1875. Schrempf is credited with inspiring Chekhov to become a doctor. He recommended Dorpat (now Tartu) to him, where lectures would be in German.

It is tempting to see Taganrog as the archetype of the provincial town of Chekhov's stories, in which despotism, conformism and sheer brainlessness produce a maddening sense of claustrophobia. 'In my childhood I had no childhood', said Chekhov later. But in fact there was a very rich 'unofficial' side to his life there. The grammar school forbade its pupils from attending the theatre, but Chekhov and his friends wangled tickets and donned elaborate disguises to see a wide repertoire including Shakespeare. Chekhov attended concerts at his better-off schoolmates' houses, acted in amateur theatricals (including Gogol's *The Government Inspector* – he played the Mayor), improvised comic sketches in the family home, produced a manuscript magazine called 'The Hiccup', caught and sold wild birds, and wrote humorous verse. Moreover, under its regimented surface Taganrog's life was far from dull: smuggling was rife, girls were sometimes snatched off the street for the Turkish harems, there were underground revolutionary cells with occasional shootouts, and wives eloped with visiting celebrities.

Finally, apart from its native Russian, Ukrainian and Yiddish, on the streets of Taganrog you could hear the languages of the major European maritime nations, as their ships still anchored in the large, silting up bay and sailors came ashore. When Chekhov fished off Taganrog's harbour wall, he was looking out to the world.

Youth: 'Fatherlessness'
1876—9

The extension of the railway through the steppe to Taganrog ruined tradesmen like Pavel Chekhov who had supplied the farmers and waggoners of the town's hinterland. He fell behind with his loan repayments and on 23rd April 1876 secretly fled to Moscow to avoid the debtors' prison. There began what has been described as 'the most mysterious part of Chekhov's biography'.

To prevent the family from being evicted, Anton encouraged their long-standing lodger, Gavriil Selivanov, to settle in court with some of his father's creditors, which effectively gave Selivanov possession of the house for 500 roubles, about £4500. This has been seen as the prototype of Lopakhin's 'usurpation' in *The Cherry Orchard*. But on several subsequent occasions Selivanov offered to sell the house back to the Chekhovs for the same price, and Chekhov remained on good terms with him for the rest of his life. In return for his initiative, when Evgeniia and her other children left for Moscow Anton received free board and lodging at Selivanov's and long holidays with the latter's relations in the steppe, but also had to tutor Selivanov's nephew and niece, which he did well. Anton's modus vivendi with the Selivanovs exemplifies his early emotional intelligence.

His next task was to prevent belongings from being seized by creditors, to sell them, and discreetly despatch the proceeds to Moscow. He also maximised his income by taking on private pupils all over Taganrog. He received heart-tugging letters from his mother describing their life on the breadline. In a letter of April 1877 to his cousin Chokhov in Moscow he reveals that he corresponds with his mother 'secretly, away from the rest', that 'nothing in the world' is dearer to him than her. In November of that year his father got a job with a Moscow merchant, Gavrilov, and lived mainly on site.

Although in this period Chekhov could not always pay his school fees – and therefore could not attend school – from 1876 he never again stayed down a year and his marks steadily improved. He joined Taganrog Public Library and borrowed hundreds of books, especially Russian and European classics. Despite his family responsibilities and intensive tutoring, Anton had more free time than before because he no longer had to serve in the shop or obsessively attend church. He began to write more 'professionally'. On 4th March 1877 the 'post-box' of a Moscow humorous weekly, *The Alarm-Clock*, announced that it would not be publishing the poems submitted by 'Nettle', a pseudonym used at the time by Chekhov. In July, another humorous paper, *The Dragonfly*, published a four-line epigram 'To Jobbing Actors', which is Chekhov's first known publication. Another short poem followed in September, but in later life Chekhov himself seems to have regarded the prose piece 'Who's to Pay' (2nd November 1878) as his debut in print. It is a perfect little dialogue between two 'dandies', Aleksandr and Nikolai, in a restaurant, and could have been based on Chekhov's visit to Moscow the previous year. All three miniatures were signed 'Youthful Hermit' in the style of the ecclesiastical sobriquets Chekhov adopted in his family.

Anton sent material to his brother Aleksandr to place in the humorous weeklies whose offices Aleksandr himself frequented. A letter from Aleksandr dated 14th October 1878 reveals that Anton had also sent him two manuscript plays – a 'drama' and a 'vaudeville'. Of the first, Aleksandr wrote: 'You ask me about "fatherlessness"… There are two scenes in "fatherlessness" which are the work of genius, if you like, but on the whole it's an unforgivable, if innocent, fraud.' Aleksandr's punctuation suggests that 'fatherlessness' is not the title of the play but an all-pervading theme; and one cannot deny this about the manuscript that was removed by the Bolsheviks from Chekhov's sister's bank safe, published in 1923, and has fathered versions with titles as varied as *Platonov* (after the protagonist), *Don Juan in the Russian Manner*, and *Wild Honey*. This play is 226 pages long in manuscript, has no title-page, and would take eight hours to perform uncut. It is a fusion of every topical and Taganrogian theme Chekhov could think of, from young radicals 'going to the people' in 1874, to the impoverishment of the gentry, women's emancipation, and the role of Jews in Russian society. Undercutting all of these, however, is the dysfunctionality of families: the young hero and heroine lack fathers to guide them morally, their fathers' whole generation is compromised by the corruption it perpetrated in the Crimean War, and most of the other characters might as well have no fathers for all the example they set them.

If *Platonov* is the play Chekhov sent his brother in 1878, it was a remarkable achievement for an eighteen year old and promised great things. Obviously it was so long that it resembled more a Russian novel. It was also more padded, tendentious and lubricious than one ever thinks of mature Chekhov. Yet the dialogue is cracklingly alive and all the characters well differentiated. It was an 'idea-soaked' melodrama, but an unmistakably comic one.

During his three poorly documented years alone in Taganrog, Chekhov enjoyed an unprecedented freedom. This worried his parents: 'We fear for you, that in our absence you may corrupt your morality, there's no-one to watch you, how you are living, and a young man's will can ruin him.' Later in life Chekhov implied that he had his first sexual experience at the age of thirteen. In 1877 he shocked his eldest brother Aleksandr by arguing in favour of polygamy. Yet in the same year he said that he had 'made all the girls cast their moorings' from him.

The evidence is that Chekhov's enforced free fall concentrated his mind on deciding for himself how he should live, what principles he needed to develop in himself if he was to survive and fulfil himself. Above all, he seems to have opted for common sense and hard work. His mother and even his father turned to him for advice, as he was capable of analysing a problem, proposing a solution, and carrying it through. He was so focussed on achieving financial independence that he managed to send his parents some of his own earnings as a tutor. Recurrent themes of his letters at this time are 'respect' and 'comforting'. His father and mother were 'the only people in the wide world for whom I will always do anything. If ever I stand high, it will be thanks to them; they are splendid people and their boundless love of their children alone puts them above all praise'. The strength of his bond with his mother lay in his readiness to comfort her, and he urged others to do the same. He discovered for himself the dignity of the individual, which had previously been smothered by his father's tyranny.

But the most important thing Chekhov learnt to value was freedom itself – the ability to make choices as an individual and act them out. In a famous letter written ten years later, he described this process of self-liberation:

Write a story about a young man – the son of a serf, a former shop-minder, chorister, schoolboy and student, brought up to grovel before rank, kiss priests' hands, and kowtow to the ideas of others, giving thanks for every crust of bread, frequently being flogged, trudging the rounds as a tutor without galoshes, brawling, tormenting animals, enjoying dinner at the houses of well-off relations, dissembling before God and man for no reason whatsoever, merely from a sense of his own inferiority – and write how this young man squeezes the slave out of himself drop by drop, and how, waking up one fine morning, he finds that the blood running in his veins is no longer the blood of a slave, but that of a real human being...

Robust intelligence, unremitting hard work, an ability to meet people 'where they are', empathy and independence, became permanent elements of Chekhov's character.

In the summer of 1879 he took his school-leaving examinations. He had to pass all of them to obtain his certificate, and he had to obtain his certificate if he was to go to university and avoid conscription. He scored five out of five for Religious Knowledge, German and Geography, four for Russian Essay, Logic, and History, but nearly failed a Maths oral. His general conduct at the school was assessed as 'excellent'. On 2nd August he was issued with an 'internal passport' that recorded him as nearly six foot tall, with reddish hair, hazel eyes, and a 'clear' complexion. He had large, long hands. A friend described him at this time as slim, handsome, with a 'wonderful smile which he retained all his life'.

Early Career: Pseudonymously Speaking
1880–5

When Chekhov walked into his parents' basement flat on the Grachevka, an infamously sordid street in central Moscow, on 8th August 1879, he brought with him several assets. He was accompanied by two school-friends, who were also to become doctors and who paid his mother as lodgers. He had won a scholarship from Taganrog Council worth 300 roubles a year (his father only earned 360), of which 100 was paid to him within weeks. Above all, he was bursting with energy. The Faculty of Medicine at Moscow University had an outstanding reputation and 'particularly in his first two years', according to a contemporary, Chekhov 'worked hard and achieved high marks'. In his brother Mikhail's words, 'since our father was living at Gavrilov's, Anton became de facto head of the household. His will became the dominant one'.

He very soon submitted short prose pieces to the humorous weeklies. On 9th March 1880 the St Petersburg *Dragonfly* printed his 'A Letter from a Don Landowner Stepan Vladimirovich N to his Learned Neighbour Friedrich', signed '...v', which is generally regarded as Chekhov's first published 'story'. It is a blend of parody of his grandfather's letter style and the 'lectures-in-character' that Chekhov had improvised before his family in Taganrog. On the next page was his 'What Do You Most Commonly Find in Novels, Short Stories &c?', which was a distillation of clichés including 'blonde goodies and red-headed baddies' and 'a dog that can do everything short of talk'. It was signed 'Antosha'. His next publication, in May, was a fully-fledged comic story signed 'Chekhonte'. Together these made the pseudonym by which, among scores of others, Chekhov was to become best known during the next five years: Antosha Chekhonte, the nickname given him at school by his teacher Father Pokrovskii.

Humorous papers like *The Dragonfly*, *The Alarm-Clock* and *The Spectator* were some of the most ephemeral publications in Russia, although they used the latest technology to reproduce coloured drawings by talented illustrators and sold well, mainly to middleclass young men. They were subject to censorship, so avoided satire, but in any case the latter was not what their readers wanted. 'Everyone cracked jokes, playful wit was all the rage', wrote a colleague of Antosha Chekhonte's. Subjects tended to reflect the seasons, the social calendar and topical events. There were stock types – the young man looking for a wife, the mother-in-law, awesome bosses, country bumpkins – but any number of genres, from the *stsenka*, a dramatic sketch, to parodies of popular writers, 'letters-in-character', joke advertisements and calendars, very short stories, novelettes, gossip, and captions to cartoons. In 1880 *The Dragonfly* paid Chekhov five kopecks a line of print.

It was a hard school for a writer, not least because the editors were brutally frank. By the end of 1880 *The Dragonfly* was accusing Chekhov of worn-out themes, 'vacuous logorrhoea' and 'having withered before you've bloomed'. Chekhov strove to be compact, versatile and entertaining. To produce this varied fare week in week out was, as he wrote to Aleksandr, to become a journalist. All it had brought him so far was 'a nervous tic' and he was determined not to 'die a journalist'.

Meanwhile, he revised his epic about 'fatherlessness'. He may have thought of this as his 'serious' writing and the work that would launch his 'real' literary career. A bluffer in the theatre world seems to have encouraged him to submit it to Ermolova, one of Moscow's top actresses. Chekhov rewrote large amounts in different-coloured pencils, stuck on patches, drafted a note to Ermolova on his manuscript, and then paid his sixteen year old brother Mikhail to make a fair copy. Presumably this is the one that was submitted to Ermolova, rejected, and according to Mikhail torn up by Anton. Whether Ermolova read, or even personally received this script, may never be known.

Quite apart from its dramatic problems, the play would have been banned by the censor. Its criticism of the conduct of the Crimean War, the fact that Platonov was a radical, and the sexual promiscuity pervading it, would have been taboo, especially after Alexander II, the 'tsar-liberator' of the serfs, was killed by a terrorist on 1st March 1881 and his heir's chief ideologist, Pobedonostsev, cracked down on public discourse across the media. The young Chekhov was surprisingly oppositional and tendentious. In Taganrog he had read all the radical writers of the 1860s – Herzen, Nekrasov, Dobroliubov, Pisemskii – and possibly regarded their *engagement* as what made a Russian writer. In 1882, at the All-Russian Exhibition in Moscow, when news broke of the Kukuevka railway accident, Chekhov exclaimed, 'Such disasters could only happen in our swinish Russia', and was threatened with arrest.

Another feature of Chekhonte that one does not associate with Chekhov is what in Russian is called *zador* and *zadiratel'nyi smekh*. The first may be rendered as 'bumptiousness', the second as 'brash mockery'. Supreme youthful exuberance swept fairness and taste before it. Thus over a two-page spread in *The Spectator* of November 1881, brilliant caricatures by Nikolai Chekhov illustrated 'The Wedding Season' and Anton's captions dismissed each member of the wedding party: '**The groom**:... Exquisitely graceful, gracefully exquisite, and... as thick as a plank... Marrying for the dowry. **The bride's father**: Drinks like a fish and is in love with next door's cook.' Unfortunately, earlier that year Nikolai and Anton had attended a relative's wedding in Taganrog and those present now recognised themselves in print. They were deeply hurt. Some of them broke off relations with the two for several years. Anton, however, neither apologised nor could see what the fuss was about. His *zador* was unstoppable.

Altogether, Chekhov's Moscow debut as a writer was disastrous. Nine months after starting with *The Dragonfly*, he had had enough of its editors' comments and dropped them. It took him nine months to find a new home in *The Spectator*. His play had fallen flat. In 1882 his first collection of stories, *Mischief*, was rejected by the censor. He did not give up. At *The Spectator* Nikolai became in-house artist and Anton in-house writer, but Anton also spread his work over a riot of Moscow publications with names like *The Minute*, *The Alarm-Clock*, *Light and Dark*, and *Talk of the World*. Chekhov's network in Moscow journalism grew ever wider and he himself more prolific. He even won a bet with one editor that he could write a novelette serialised over three months, which readers would believe was by the Hungarian bestseller Mór Jókai.

In late 1882 Chekhov got his first break: he was invited by Nikolai Leikin to contribute to his Petersburg humorous weekly *Splinters*. This was the best comic sheet in the country. In the words of Chekhonte's colleague, the poetaster Liodor Pal´min, it was 'honest and admirably liberal'. Moreover, it paid eight kopecks a line. Leikin was a workaholic, graphomaniacal, and in Chekhov's words 'bourgeois to the marrow', but he probably helped Chekhov more than any other editor.

From slow beginnings, Chekhov rose to contributing three or four items weekly to *Splinters*. In 1883, when seventy-three of his eclectic contributions were published in the paper, he produced some of his first classic works. 'The Death of a Civil Servant' (2nd July 1883) evokes Kafkaesque fear inside a monolithic state. At the same time, it turned upside down the mawkish Russian literary cliché of the 'oppressed little man'. In the style of the comic weeklies, the protagonist's name means roughly Maggotkin. He is at the bottom of the hierarchy of

Tsarist bureaucracy – which was organised in fourteen ranks. To his horror, he sneezes on the pate of an elderly gentleman sitting in front of him at the operetta, who turns out to be General Splutterov, a 'Number 2 in the Ministry of Communications'. The Number 14 apologises and the Number 2 accepts his apology. Maggotkin, however, is so terrified by the thought of his 'disrespect' that he harasses the general for days with his apologies until the latter explodes at him, whereupon Maggotkin staggered home, 'without taking off his uniform lay down on the sofa, and... died'.

Similarly, 'The Daughter of Albion' (13th August 1883) appears at first to present 'brash' comic types of the Russian landowner and the English governess, but turns out to be concerned with a discreet basic value – human dignity. 'Miss Tvice' and her employer, Griabov, are fishing by a stream when they are joined by Griabov's friend. Griabov loudly ridicules to the latter everything about Miss Tvice, since she understands no Russian. Finally, to his friend's consternation, Griabov strips in front of Miss Tvice and wades into the water to free his line. A 'haughty, contemptuous smile' passes over Miss Tvice's 'yellow face'. 'She might at least show some embarrassment, the hussy!' says Griabov, emerging from the water. 'Look at those eyebrows twitching!... She's above the crowd! Ha, ha, ha! She doesn't even regard us as human beings!... Bit different from England, eh?!' But the joke is on Griabov and the last sentence has become proverbial in Russia as a self-criticism.

Another early classic, 'Minds in Ferment' (16th June 1884), illustrates how carefully Leikin had to handle the censor and how this could aggravate Chekhov's relations with him. In this story, set in a sleepy Russian town, two respectable citizens stand in the street watching a cloud of starlings descend on a cleric's orchard in the distance. Passers-by stop and stare, and before long a crowd has gathered. An officious policeman arrests the 'guilty parties', who are jailed 'for a week or so' without trial. The censor objected to Chekhov's original title, 'Minds in Turmoil', and to the use of 'turmoil' elsewhere, as it was a term associated with uprising and could suggest that the story referred to the suspension of rights of assembly under Alexander III. Leikin therefore came up with 'Ferment', inserted at the end 'And it was all caused by a flock of starlings', and the story got through. However, for Chekhov this insertion 'ruined the whole point', namely the absurdity of no-one knowing the 'cause' of the 'riot' in the first place.

The year 1884 saw Chekhov advance on several fronts. In May he took his finals. At the beginning of June he brought out *Tales of Melpomene*, a collection of stories that the censor passed because they concentrated on the world of the theatre and avoided 'politics'. But Melpomene is the Muse of Tragedy and nearly all the stories have dark undertones. The book was self-published but eventually made a profit. In the middle of June Chekhov qualified as a general practitioner and left for Voskresensk, about forty miles north of Moscow, where he could work all summer as a district doctor and write, whilst his family stayed nearby at his schoolmaster brother Ivan's. In July Anton completed his longest ever piece of fiction, *The Hunt Murder*, an ingenious half-spoof detective novel that ran in the *Daily News* until April 1885.

Probably because he put his medicine first, in 1884 Chekhov wrote much less for *Splinters* than the previous year. Even so, 'A. Chekhonte' and 'The Man Without Spleen' became the most dependable and popular contributor after Leikin himself.

Chekhov's most onerous tasks for Leikin were writing the captions around which cartoons would be drawn, and composing 'Splinters of Moscow Life', a column of news stories and tittle-tattle. He found the latter more difficult than fiction, but in November 1884 it led to him being invited by the daily *Petersburg Newspaper* to report a sensational fraud trial in Moscow. Being a court reporter was a gruelling daily routine. After a fortnight, Chekhov had a haemorrhage from one lung that continued for three days. He dismissed it to Leikin as 'a small burst blood vessel', but he knew it could be tuberculosis. This did not mean it was 'hereditary' or 'terminal'. The most common cause of TB was dark, damp, overcrowded accommodation, and the Chekhovs had plenty of that. Several of Chekhov's family had bouts of tuberculosis and lived to make old bones. Chekhov's own urban lifestyle, however, was much more frenetic and in his journalist years he smoked cigarettes heavily.

In 1885 Chekhov continued to turn out 'Splinters of Moscow Life' and wrote over fifty items for Leikin in the usual motley of genres. However, the proportion of 'journalism' in his total output began to decline, because in May he was taken on by the *Petersburg Newspaper* to contribute a story every Monday. In the same month, Chekhov took himself and his family off to Babkino, near Voskresensk, where they stayed for a long summer in a spacious dacha owned by the Kiselevs, local impoverished aristocrats. The Kiselevs provided Chekhov with his first sustained experience of upper-class and 'intellectual' life. Babkino's ambience was to influence *Ivanov* and even *Three Sisters*, but in the summer of 1885 it inspired a series of short masterpieces, both comic and more serious, which were published in the *Petersburg Newspaper*.

'The Burbot' (1st July 1885) was based on a real incident at Babkino. Two carpenters building a bathing-hut on the river try to extract a monster burbot that has wedged itself among the roots of an overhanging willow. The story was subtitled 'A Scene' and a brilliant dramatic double-act evolves in demotic Russian. An ancient one-eyed herdsman leaves his animals and swims across to help. As the men pull and push the fish, horses, sheep and cows invade the master's garden and he comes out to investigate. Driven by the thought of the fish's fine meat on his table, he strips and joins in. Eventually he pulls it out and 'for a whole minute' everyone contemplates the wonderful creature, particularly its pregnant-looking liver, which was a great delicacy. Then with one writhe it is in the water and away... We are left with a memory of supreme vitality and fecundity.

A fortnight later, the *Petersburg Newspaper* published 'The Huntsman'. This too evoked high summer in the Russian countryside sparingly, with precise selected images, but its focus is on a relationship. Egor, a peasant shooter retained by one of the gentry, is ambling along with his dog and gun when he comes across Pelageia, a peasant woman, cutting rye. They are, in fact, married, but Egor regards it as a forced marriage and does not live with her. Pelageia, however, dotes on him. He condescends to sit down briefly and talk. She soon suggests that his passion, hunting, is not a real job and he should return to the land and her. He counters, 'Once that free spirit's got into a man, there's no winkling it out… You're a woman, you don't understand'. Their dialogue, which ends with her watching him disappear in the distance, stirs the very depths of communicability between the sexes, and brings the reader to that state of near-tears-without-sentiment that is authentically 'Chekhovian'. In faraway Petersburg the elder writer Grigorovich read 'The Huntsman' and rushed round with it to the editorial offices of *New Times* to persuade its proprietor, Aleksei Suvorin, to take Chekhov on.

A week later, the *Petersburg Newspaper* published 'The Malefactor', another story concerning fish (Chekhov loved angling). An illiterate peasant is up before the examining magistrate accused of unscrewing nuts from railway sleepers to use as sinkers. He does not deny it: '"Wouldn't have been unscrewing it if I hadn't needed it, would I?" croaks Denis, squinting at the ceiling.' His explanation of why he 'needs' it is a disquisition to the 'stupid' magistrate on what every peasant knows – the different ways of catching different fish. Conversely, the magistrate attempts to make the peasant understand why his action is illegal; but in vain. Both are locked in their own worlds, incapable of going beyond themselves to understand the other. 'Communication' fails.

Other tragi-comic masterpieces of 'non-communication' that Chekhov wrote in the autumn of 1885 included 'Sergeant Prishibeev' and 'The Misfortune' (or 'Grief'). In the latter, a peasant is taking his wife to hospital lying on a sledge through a blizzard, and as he drives the horse on he pours out to her his regrets for how he has treated her in the past – but she is already dead. Pal´min wrote to Chekhov that it was the best thing he had written: 'Here the grim and the comical are intertwined, as in peasant life.'

By the end of 1885 Chekhov was acquiring a more discerning readership outside the humorous press. But it was not clear how he could build on this, and his personal life was as insecure as ever. After returning from Babkino, the family moved twice within Moscow before Christmas. Chekhov's income was not much more than today's minimum wage. In November he had no money to buy firewood. If he had devoted himself full time to medicine in Moscow, and abandoned writing, he would have been quite well-off. If he had devoted himself full time to writing he would not remotely have been able to support his six-member family. As it was, many of his patients were acquaintances from Moscow's artistic world and did not pay him at all! Moreover, Chekhov's strengths as a doctor were diagnosis, empathy, and personal commitment, which made medical failure particularly stressful for him. At the end of the year he treated a mother and three sisters for typhus and one of them died gripping his hand. According to Mikhail Chekhov, at this point Anton took his doctor's plate down and 'decided once and for all to devote himself to literature'. It was inconceivable for him to do this at one stroke, however, and there is evidence that through the 1880s Chekhov toyed with doing a Ph.D. and going into academic medicine.

It had become clear to Chekhov that the path to a literary career lay through St Petersburg. Obviously, his main two literary sources of income were already there. Culturally, Moscow was a comparative backwater. Almost all of Russia's recent great writers had worked in Petersburg: Nekrasov (d. 1877), Dostoevsky (d. 1881), Turgenev (d. 1883), and Leskov (still active). At long last, on 10th December 1885, Chekhov took the train to the capital.

From Journalist to Writer
1886–9

'My whole stay was a series of sheer delights', wrote Chekhov to Leikin on his return to Moscow a fortnight later, but it was less than the truth. He had stayed in some style with Leikin, who accompanied him everywhere, but Leikin was disdained in St Petersburg's higher literary circles. Suvorin, Grigorovich and Khudekov (editor of the *Petersburg Newspaper*) were lukewarm towards Chekhov as a Leikin protégé, and Leikin's presence signalled that he was determined to hang on to Chekhov as a stalwart contributor. The only practical outcome seemed to be Leikin's own proposal that *Splinters* publish Chekhov's next book.

In the New Year, however, things moved fast. Kurepin, a previous editor of *The Alarm-Clock*, arrived in Moscow with instructions from Suvorin to negotiate Chekhov's contributing a Saturday story to *New Times* at twelve kopecks a line. Chekhov agreed, but kept the news from Leikin for as long as possible.

In February, Chekhov wrote his first story for *New Times*, 'The Requiem'. It was perfectly tailored to the newspaper's tastes: robustly humorous and 'tacky'. Chekhov had, in fact, a deserved reputation among journalists for salaciousness (most notoriously, a story of 1883 concerned voyeurs observing a newly wed couple's first night), and the heroines of his next two stories for Suvorin ('The Witch' and 'Agaf'ia') were also women who 'wandered'. Before 'The Requiem' was published Suvorin telegrammed Chekhov asking for permission to sign his contributions with Chekhov's real name. The point was not so much that 'Antosha Chekhonte' was associated with humour as that it was virtually the property of *Splinters* and its parent *Petersburg Newspaper*. But Suvorin was counting on more serious work than Chekhov had ever produced and felt that it would be worthy of his full name. Chekhov, however, intended to keep 'Anton Chekhov' for medical publications. They reached a compromise: he would write under the name 'An. Chekhov', to distinguish him from Aleksandr, who still wrote for the humorous press.

In March Chekhov received a long letter from Dmitrii Grigorovich, one-time friend of Dostoevsky and Turgenev, and Petersburg's most 'distinguished' living writer. He praised the 'truthfulness' of Chekhov's character portrayals and descriptions of nature. 'You have *real* talent', he wrote. 'I am sure it is your vocation to write several superb, truly artistic works. You will be committing a great sin if you don't fulfil these expectations.' To do so, Chekhov should give up 'deadline work' for the lesser press, write a 'highly thought-out and polished' extended work, and 'after your recent stories in *New Times* and the success of "The Huntsman", abandon the pseudonym Chekhonte'.

Grigorovich's letter was a sensational endorsement of Chekhov's progress in print since 1880. Nevertheless, Chekhov wrote in his emotional reply, of the twenty or so writers he knew in Moscow he could not think of one who had 'read me or looks upon me as an artist'. If he were to read to Moscow's 'literary circle' anything from Grigorovich's letter, they would 'laugh in my face'. He accepted all Grigorovich's advice but said that it was too late to put his 'real name' on the title page of his new book. Hyperbolically, he said that until now he had written his stories 'the way journalists report fires... mechanically, half-unconsciously'. He added, however, that he had always 'tried not to waste on a story images and whole pictures that were dear to me and that I, God knows why, saved up and carefully hid' – suggesting again that he had his own agenda as a writer.

Although Chekhov wrote prolifically for *Splinters* and the *Petersburg Newspaper* in 1886, and began to get into his stride with *New Times*, he consistently hit higher artistic levels. 'Kids' displayed an uncanny knowledge of children's speech and psychology. In 'Aniuta' a young lower-class woman is passed around a group of students who use her as an artist's model or anatomical skeleton, and she lives with one who is about to dump her. The engendered sense of depersonalisation and suppressed tears is unbearable. In 'Easter Night' Chekhov used his profound knowledge of ecclesiastical life and liturgy to portray a poet in prose – a monk who composed canticles and has just died – together with the love of his surviving male friend. Chekhov's range of subject was becoming extraordinary. 'Romance with Double-Bass' was a pastoral farce with nudity. 'The Chorus-Girl' explores all the humiliation of the demimonde and was regarded by Tolstoy as one of Chekhov's very best stories. 'The Spongers' broached animal rights. Even Leikin praised 'The Objet d'Art' as one of the funniest stories Chekhov had written.

Yet with all these works we must be wary of generalising about 'early Chekhov'. Many of them were crucially tweaked by Chekhov throughout his life. For example, in 1886 the famous 'Little Joke' ended with a wedding, but the 'Chekhovian' essence of the story as we know it today (as revised in 1899) is that the hero funks a proposal and regrets it all his life. Hence, the concept 'early Chekhov' is relativistic: there is the fictive 'early Chekhov' of the last completed versions, and the strictly chronological early Chekhov reconstructed by scholars.

In May 1886 Chekhov's *Motley Tales* came out, containing seventy-seven very varied works. It was well received in short notices for its hilarity and human warmth. However, one Skabichevskii in a 'serious' journal accused Chekhov of being a 'newspaper clown' and predicted that he would die 'completely forgotten in a ditch'. The book subsequently went through fourteen editions.

The most startling event in Anton's life in 1886 was his 'engagement' to Dunia (Evdokiia) Efros. He informed his St Petersburg confidant Viktor Bilibin of this event, but whether he told anyone else is unclear. Since living in Moscow, Chekhov had visited prostitutes, consorted with chorus girls, and had a two-year affair with a Jewess, Natal'ia Gol'den. Efros was also Jewish. According to Chekhov, she bitterly resented the legal requirement to convert to Orthodoxy if she wanted to marry a Russian (a theme of *Ivanov* the following year), and the 'engagement' was soon off. She was a fellow student of Chekhov's sister Mariia (Masha) and 'respectable'. Chekhov's relationships with his sister's friends were usually unconsummated. An exception was Ol'ga Kundasova, an oval-faced *émancipée* and astronomer whom he met at the end of this year and partly portrayed as Rassudina in 'Three Years'. In a celebrated letter in March 1886 Chekhov had written that 'educated people' endeavour 'as far as possible to tame and ennoble the sexual instinct'.

The letter was occasioned by what was becoming a millstone for Chekhov: his elder brothers' dissolute and self-indulgent behaviour. Aleksandr had a succession of jobs in Customs and Excise, but blew his salary on drinking bouts. In 1886 he suffered alcoholic blindness and dumped himself and his illegitimate family on the Moscow Chekhovs whilst he dried out. He continued to exploit Anton's success to place his own passé stories about 'oppressed clerks and husbands' (Leikin). Nikolai, meanwhile, was addicted to women, drink and the Bohemian lifestyle. He took advances from Anton's artistic contacts for work that he never completed. In another attempt to return Nikolai to the family, Anton wrote to him acknowledging his virtues but accusing him of egocentricity. He enumerated 'conditions that educated people must satisfy'. They included 'respecting the human person', 'showing compassion not just to beggars and cats', 'respecting other people's property and therefore paying one's debts', 'never lying, even about little things', and 'respecting one's own talent'. Under each heading, Chekhov explained what he meant. It has been speculated that this is an ethical code that Chekhov himself had fought to acquire as he moved onwards and upwards. The theme running through it is self-control.

Domestically, it was a great advance when in September 1886 the Chekhovs rented a small Moscow house that they lived in for the next four years. This was the surgeon Korneev's property on Sadovo-Kudrinskaia road, which cost about £125 a week and was described by Chekhov as 'a red chest of drawers'. It is now a museum.

Here Chekhov occasionally practised as a doctor, but above all could concentrate on writing. The pattern established itself of a Saturday story for *New Times*, a Monday/Friday one for the *Petersburg Newspaper*, and ever less for *Splinters*. Chekhov wrote almost as much in 1887 – over 500 pages of print – as the previous year, but there were no 'trifles' amongst his output now, it was nearly all first-class short stories each encapsulating a fresh subject and world. In 'The Beggar' (19th January) Chekhov polemicised humorously with Tolstoy's moralistic approach to Moscow's underclass. In 'Enemies' (20th January) he explored the Jungian ambivalence of powerful immediate experiences: authentic grief fills a doctor first with sanctimoniousness, then hatred. Both 'Polly' (2nd February) and 'Little Vera' (21st February) were destined to become classic Chekhovian 'non-love' stories.

On 10th February 1887, however, Chekhov wrote to Suvorin that 'domestic matters' were sapping his creative energy and he was planning a trip to southern Russia to 'refresh my memory of things that have begun to fade' – evidence, perhaps, that he was preparing for the 'long work' that Grigorovich and others urged him to produce. But in March his brother Aleksandr telegrammed to say he was dangerously ill and Anton left for Petersburg. He found the city in the grip of a typhoid epidemic. His brother was 'perfectly well', but his common-law wife had mild abdominal typhoid, which Chekhov treated. Come what may, Anton wrote to a friend, he was going south as his nerves 'won't take any more'. He returned to Moscow, where he wrote the virtually infectious story 'Typhus', was told that his brother Nikolai was coughing blood and Aleksandr's whole family in hospital, and on 2nd April left for Taganrog.

The journey was made possible by a generous advance from Suvorin, but whilst he was away Chekhov wrote as Chekhonte for the less demanding *Petersburg Newspaper*. The 'Asiatic' Taganrog appalled him. He was fêted by relations whom he had not seen for six years, old school-friends, and many women. He revisited his steppe haunts, sometimes riding far on horseback. After Easter he stayed at the Sviatye Gory monastery south of Khar'kov, which accommodated 15,000 pilgrims for Summer St Nicholas Day. A series of informers were attached to Chekhov to fathom the purpose of his peregrinations. He returned to Moscow on 17th May and next day left for Babkino.

It was a tense summer for Chekhov. When he was not writing, he was standing in as a zemstvo (rural council) doctor, or treating the local peasants free. By 22nd May he had written 'Fortune' for *New Times*, based on his recent journey. It caused a sensation. It was, in Chekhov's words, a 'quasi-symphony' of motifs, voices and narrative tempi, on a philosophical theme dear to the Russian heart: can humans be happy? According to Aleksandr, in the restaurants of St Petersburg's Nevskii Avenue this copy of *New Times* was displayed for over a week, as everyone wanted to read it. In July, *New Times* published another 'steppe story', 'The Tumbleweed', based on a wandering Jew he had met on his monastery visit, and this too stirred minds. Meanwhile, Chekhov's next book of published stories, *In the Twilight*, was ready to appear but was waiting for Suvorin – who had retired to his dacha in deep depression following the suicide of one of his sons – to price it. Nikolai Chekhov's physical condition worsened. It rained almost every day. On 29th August the superb 'Reed-Pipe' was printed in *New Times*, a story set precisely in such weather and centred on an old peasant who foretells ecological disaster. On 2nd September Chekhov moved back to Moscow.

Immediately, he had his first documented bout of 'black dog'. In a long letter to Aleksandr he complained that he was lonely, had no-one to talk to, was surrounded by compulsive lying and vulgarity, had no money even to buy clothes, could not work, and 'if fate doesn't become kinder' might commit suicide. The most uncharacteristic element here is the statement that he could not work. But Aleksandr replied perceptively, 'I can believe it. You need to live, not work. You've worked yourself into the ground. The south inspired you and fired you up, but that wasn't enough.' Chekhov was also depressed by *New Times*'s journalism (for example its attacks on Darwin) and by a major review of his new book that described it as 'questions without answers, answers without questions, stories without a beginning or end, plots without dénouements'. In the past year he had written non-stop, yet he still could not pay his rent.

Chekhov's acquaintance with depression undoubtedly assisted him in his new project: his first publicly acknowledged full-length play, *Ivanov*. The commission was a bolt from the blue. He had been rubbishing a new play at the best private theatre in Moscow, when its manager, Fedor Korsh, challenged him to write a better one. Korsh's theatre was best known for its humorous entertainment and Chekhov subtitled *Ivanov* 'A Comedy'. He hung a notice 'Very Busy' on his study door and completed the play in ten days. Now he was on a high: 'everyone' liked the play, Korsh could not find in it 'a single mistake or transgression against the stage', and the star actor Davydov loved the lead role. However, the play was hardly an unalloyed comedy. As with his teenage effort, Chekhov was attempting to create a 'significant literary type' that said something about the state of Russia, and he ended each act with 'a punch in the face'. Conversely, at the close of the play, after being melodramatically insulted, Ivanov died on a sofa of a heart attack amidst lines worthy of a farce.

The first night, 19th November 1887, was what many present called a *skandal* (uproar). The lyrical first act went well, despite the fact that only the two leads knew their lines. There were many people onstage in the second act, things became muddled, but still it was well received. The third act, building slowly to the play's climax, Ivanov's verbal abuse of his Jewish wife, was a huge success and Chekhov took three company bows. In this version, however, the last act was in two halves. The long scene change broke the audience's concentration. Some of the performers now acted drunk and at least one really was. In Chekhov's account, the audience were 'perplexed', did not 'understand' Ivanov's death, and at the curtain call some 'blatantly hissed' but were drowned out by others clapping and stamping. His brother Mikhail claimed that at the end the audience 'sprang from their seats' and a fight broke out in the gallery between the hissers and the applauders. Basically what seems to have happened is that the younger part of the audience were gripped by what they recognised as a truthful portrayal of their contemporaries in the depressed Russia of the times, and the rest were as outraged by its 'immoral', 'cynical' realism as many of the reviewers. But no-one could deny that Chekhov had created a theatrical stir. Some theatregoers said they had never heard so many arguments after a play.

Ivanov had only three performances, but was immediately taken up by the provinces. Four days later Chekhov left for nearly a month in Petersburg. Suvorin was smitten by *Ivanov* and engaged Chekhov in long conversations about it. Chekhov met Mikhailovskii, Korolenko and Uspenskii, the literary team of the 'thick journal' *Northern Herald*. He was passed from one fan to another: the older poets Polonskii and Pleshcheev, the young prose writers Leont´ev, Barentsevich and Bilibin, the painter Repin. Several of these men found Chekhov's charm, indeed his feminine side, irresistible. As Leont´ev put it, they were 'intoxicated' by him. On 5th December 1887 Chekhov's last story as a regular contributor appeared in *Splinters*, and on 15th December his haunting prose elegy 'The Kiss' appeared in *New Times*. The year, it seemed, had ended in triumph.

The mystery, however, is what had happened to the 'novel' Chekhov was writing in 1887. In July he recounted the first chapter to a 'disciple' writer, Lazarev-Gruzinskii. Its southern setting recalled *Platonov*. In October he told Aleksandr that he had 'not yet copied out' the novel, which was only 1500 newspaper lines long and which Suvorin was keen to print in *New Times*. Little more was ever heard of it. Could it have mutated into 'The Story of a Nobody', which was published in 1893 but which Chekhov said he had started in 1887, or even into the 'little trilogy' published in 1898?

The new work that Chekhov began around 1st January 1888, 'The Steppe', was not a novel, but it has been described as 'in European terms Chekhov's most modern narrative creation' (Dmitrii Likhachev), anticipating Proust and Joyce. He was all too aware how much depended upon it: it was the first work he had been invited to contribute to a 'serious', 'thick journal' and if it was successful he could publish longer works in these journals, drop the weeklies, and earn more. Clearly he had been gestating it since May 1887. He used notebooks that he had kept during his travels. He had made a special study of the 'poets' prose' of Pushkin and Lermontov, and knew Gogol's steppe descriptions well. Nevertheless, writing something so long and innovative cost him great effort. He feared he was producing 'not a picture but an encyclopaedia of the steppe'. Halfway through he had to stop to earn some money by writing the six-page tragedy 'Let Me Sleep', in which a thirteen year old childminder smothers a baby. It was almost his last story for the *Petersburg Newspaper*. By 2nd February 'The Steppe' was complete.

Its critical reception set a pattern for years to come. Professional writers like Pleshcheev, Garshin and Shchedrin were enraptured by its evocativeness, empathy and originality; common readers found its 'lyricism' irresistible. The doyen of critics, however, was Nikolai Mikhailovskii, who was coincidentally the ideological authority at the *Northern Herald* in which 'The Steppe' appeared. Mikhailovskii was the leader of Russian Populism and 'a sort of Russian combination of Darwin, Karl Marx, and Walter Lippman, an infallible oracle' (Adam B. Ulam). He wrote to Chekhov criticising 'The Steppe' for its 'inconsequentiality', which he attributed to Chekhov's association with such morally 'disoriented' publications as *New Times*. Chekhov was expected to accept this gratefully, but did not. He replied that he was not committed to an ideological 'orientation' and only Suvorin had helped him up the literary ladder. Mikhailovskii retorted that Chekhov's stories were 'directly serving evil', the correspondence broke off, and Mikhailovskii left the journal shortly after. Chekhov stayed. Many other reviewers at the time criticised 'The Steppe' for its 'inconsequentiality', 'fragmentariness' and 'unfinished' quality. It was like dismissing Seurat's paintings of the same period for not presenting continuously applied paint.

As if for light relief, Chekhov now tossed off a 'vaudeville', *The Bear*. 'Vaudevilles' on the Russian stage at this time were one-act plays lasting about half an hour, influenced by French examples but without music. Chekhov's first one-act play to pass the censor was *Swan Song*, which was written in 1887 and premiered in February 1888 with great success. This probably spurred Chekhov to write *The Bear*, but it was not cleared by the censor until seven months later. It then began its triumphant progress over the Russian stage together with *The Proposal*, written and passed for performance in the autumn of 1888. The manic absurdity of these playlets' characters is reminiscent of Ionesco in the next century. Reviewers praised this absurdity, but also noted the 'truthfulness to life' of Chekhov's vaudevilles. *The Bear*, indeed, could be said to turn on the 'Female Question' of the times: 'If women want equality', growls its hero, 'they can damned well have it – I challenge you to a duel!'

Meanwhile, through the spring and summer of 1888, Chekhov travelled. In March he was in Petersburg, cultivating his contacts at the *Northern Herald* and staying with Suvorin. A photograph of Chekhov then shows him as strikingly handsome, lightly bearded, with thick long hair swept back off his high forehead, and immaculately dressed. In May, just as Suvorin was bringing out a new volume of his stories including 'The Steppe', Chekhov left with his mother and sister for a dacha near Sumy, in Ukraine. It belonged to the Lintvarevs, a liberal upper-class family that included two daughters who were doctors. Chekhov was bowled over by the family, the 'poetical setting' by the Psel river, the fishing, the warmth, and the Ukrainian vivacity. He invited a string of Petersburg friends to stay with him, which some did. He spent a week touring Poltava province in a Gogolian carriage. On 10th July he set out alone to stay with the Suvorin family at Feodosiia on the Black Sea.

It was this contact that cemented Chekhov's friendship with Suvorin and led to him corresponding over the next ten years more frequently and frankly with Suvorin than within anyone else. 'We converse all day', Chekhov wrote to Leont´ev at the time, 'and then all night.' Suvorin was 'sensitivity incarnate', 'a self-taught man who has honed his instinct into a penetrating mind', 'a major figure'. On 23rd July Chekhov left Feodosiia with Suvorin's son Aleksei on a trip to the Caucasus that took in Sukhumi, Batum, Tiflis and Baku. On 7th August he returned to the Lintvarevs' dacha and by 3rd September the Chekhovs were back in their 'red chest of drawers' in Moscow.

That autumn, the literary worlds of both capitals were a-twitter with the news that the Academy of Sciences had awarded its Pushkin Prize to Chekhov for his book of stories *In the Twilight*. True, he had to share it with Korolenko, but the prize was the clearest public recognition that he had at last arrived as a writer. The congratulations poured in, and henceforth Chekhov's work was usually signed 'Anton Chekhov'. Yet he still had doubts about his vocation. He wrote to Suvorin that medicine was his 'lawful wife' and literature his 'mistress'. All year 'ideological' critics had attacked his writing for its 'lack of ideas'. No Russian reviewer he had read had ever helped him discover 'who' he was as a writer, indeed in Russia there was 'no literary criticism at all'.

On the personal front, things deteriorated. Although he claimed that he did not have the syndrome of tuberculosis, he was again coughing blood. He still smoked. Whilst in Petersburg in December he visited Aleksandr and was disgusted by his behaviour towards the new woman in his life, Natal'ia Gol'den, who had once been Anton's lover. On 23rd December 1888 Chekhov wrote that he was being overwhelmed by his extended family's demands on him, and even 'beginning at times to hate people, which never happened to me before'.

It was the prelude to one of the worst years in Chekhov's life. His relationship with Suvorin was at its height: Chekhov oversaw the Moscow premiere of Suvorin's play *Tat'iana Repina*, and Suvorin guided *Ivanov* through its Petersburg premiere. For this Chekhov had replaced the 1887 ending with Ivanov's suicide. Four of Petersburg's star actors – Davydov, Strepetova, Svobodin and Savina – ensured that it was a tremendous success. However, again the stress of a theatrical first night had exhausted Chekhov, he started bleeding from the throat, and within three days was back in Moscow.

The next month, Chekhov discovered that his vagrant brother Nikolai was bedridden with tuberculosis. He moved him to the Chekhov home. He explained to Masha that Nikolai ought to go to the Crimea to convalesce but they could not afford it, so he was taking him to Sumy, to the dacha they had rented the year before. Here the whole Chekhov family assembled, except for Pavel, and Nikolai Chekhov died on 13th June 1889. Even while caring for Nikolai in Moscow, Anton had been 'literally incapable of working'. Nikolai's death, the first in Chekhov's immediate family, now drained him completely.

After accompanying his mother to a monastery with an icon famous for comforting those who grieve, Chekhov set out for Odessa. His plan, agreed with Suvorin and Grigorovich, was to meet them in Vienna and tour the Tyrol. In Odessa, however, Chekhov fell in with a company from the Moscow Malyi Theatre, and got no further. Grigorovich fumed day after day waiting for Chekhov's train at a Vienna station, the Suvorins were bemused, and Chekhov blamed the telegraph service. Later he confided to Suvorin's wife that he had 'met someone, and this someone had changed his itinerary'. This was presumably Kleopatra Karatygina, a widowed actress twelve years his senior, with whom Chekhov later had an affair but who in 1889 treated him with exactly the bonhomie and mothering that he needed. Around the middle of July Chekhov told Karatygina, a Siberian, of his intention of going to Sakhalin in the Far East, asking her not to repeat this in Moscow.

In Odessa and then Yalta, Chekhov worked on *The Wood Demon* and a long first-person narrative begun the previous year; it was called first 'My Name and I' and finally 'A Boring Story'. When a local writer asked Chekhov why the central character of his new play was 'a man in love with forests', Chekhov snapped, 'Topical subject'. Chekhov also told him, 'If you've hung a pistol on the wall in the first act, it must go off in the last. Otherwise, don't hang it there.' To the *Northern Herald*'s publisher he confided that he kept having to rewrite 'whole pages' of 'A Boring Story' because they were infected with the 'revolting mood that I've not been able to shake off all summer' – death.

But since Professor Nikolai Stepanovich, the hero of 'A Boring Story', is a terminally ill narrator, Chekhov's mood may have enhanced its power. To Chekhov's surprise, when the story came out in the *Northern Herald* in November it was almost universally praised. Even Leikin, who had been unable to finish 'The Steppe', felt that 'A Boring Story' was the best thing Chekhov had written. Positive comparisons were made with Tolstoy's 'The Death of Ivan Il'ich' (1886).

Unfortunately, the premiere of *The Wood Demon* the following month was an even worse *skandal* than *Ivanov*. After the play was rejected by a repertory committee in Petersburg, Chekhov gave it to his friend Solovtsov's company in Moscow. This company had broken away from Korsh's company, who had premiered *Ivanov* and asked Chekhov for *The Wood Demon*.

A claque of Korsh's actors therefore howled the new play down and 'all those who wished Chekhov ill and envied him' joined in. The next day, Chekhov left for Babkino. Most of the reviews accused him of wilfully ignoring the 'rules of theatre' by presenting a string of 'episodes', and denied vehemently that the 'wood demon' was the play's central character.

From Babkino, Chekhov escaped on 3rd January 1890 to St Petersburg. He had in mind, however, a more extreme escape. 'I am going to Sakhalin', he wrote to Pleshcheev on 10th February. 'The decision is irrevocable.'

Siberia: A Journey to Hell
1890

As rumour of Chekhov's impending journey to Russia's penal colony in the Far East spread, the press usually described its purpose as 'to study the convicts' way of life'. But why did Chekhov want to do this? Given the political sensitivity of penal servitude, no further public explanation could be broached. This has led to some wild speculation. Was he perhaps running away from a number of attachments, including one to a married woman, that he could not handle? It has even been suggested that he was on the verge of a nervous breakdown. He hardly helped by saying that he was going because 'I feel like crossing a year or eighteen months out of my life, that's all' (why did he?). It is a prime example of how the image of Chekhov as 'elusive' could arise.

In fact, the decision to go to Sakhalin exemplifies how deeply Chekhov planned his own life and how he communicated such plans only to a handful of people he trusted. In 1903 he explained to Miroliubov that by the end of the 1880s he had had enough of the virulent attacks on him by ideological 'critics' and intended to abandon literature. His plan was to carry out research on Sakhalin, write it up as a Ph.D. thesis, and apply for an academic post in medicine – which he did, to no avail, in the late nineties. The epistolary evidence is that he divulged this plan only to Suvorin.

As it happened, the 'shit' (Chekhov's word) heaped on him by 'critics' was particularly bad in the months before he left. To a journalist who nagged him in person for presenting no 'ideals' or 'positive types' in his work, Chekhov riposted, 'My heroes are tormented people – I can hardly depict the heroes of some triumphant "idea" if such heroes don't exist in real life!' The first publication of 'A Boring Story' and its republication in a new collection called *Sombre People* brought a spate of reviews claiming that Chekhov suffered from the same failing as the story's hero, namely the lack of a 'comprehensive idea', i.e. ideology. These critics were humourless 'systemists' and nascent totalitarians. In a letter to Pleshcheev, on the contrary, Chekhov had written that he saw his hero's major failing as one of *empathy* towards the flesh and blood people around him. Finally, in March 1890, a journalist at *Russian Thought* called Chekhov in print an 'unprincipled writer'. Chekhov broke off all relations with the editor including even 'raising hats in the street'.

Suvorin, the publisher of a newspaper widely regarded as reactionary and virtually a government mouthpiece, told Chekhov that nobody 'needed' his study of Sakhalin. Chekhov defended it explicitly: 'From the books I have read so far, it's obvious that we have rotted *millions* of people in these prisons, rotted them pointlessly, irrationally, barbarically; we have herded people through the cold in fetters for thousands of miles, infected them with syphilis, depraved them, bred criminals, and blamed it all on ruddy-nosed warders.' What is most modern about Chekhov's argument in this letter is that he assigns moral responsibility for the Siberian penal system to every single Russian, including himself. 'All educated Europe', he told Suvorin, knew of this iniquity, 'but we don't care, we're not interested.' To another friend, whom he tried to persuade to accompany him, he said that penal servitude 'may be one of the most terrible absurdities that man has ever invented'. Even before he reached Sakhalin, Chekhov was arguing in travel notes published in *New Times* that Siberian penal servitude plus life exile had simply inherited the aim of capital punishment, namely 'to remove the offender from a normal human environment *forever*. 'I am deeply convinced', he wrote then, 'that in fifty to a hundred years we shall look on the fact that our punishments are life sentences with the same astonishment and embarrassment as we now look upon slitting people's nostrils or chopping a finger off their left hand.' There was nothing 'elusive', then, about either the purpose or moral impetus of Chekhov's journey.

His family and friends saw him off in a third-class carriage to Iaroslavl', 150 miles north of Moscow, on 21st April 1890. In Iaroslavl' he boarded a steamer down the Volga, accompanied for some of the way by Kundasova, and then steamed along the Kama north-eastwards to Perm', whence he travelled by train to Ekaterinburg, arriving on 28th April. Here he was informed that there would be no steamer from Tiumen' to Tomsk for three weeks, so he would have to cover that thousand miles by cart! He arrived by train in Tiumen' on 3rd May.

The overland journey to Tomsk was an extreme test for Chekhov. It was the coldest Siberian 'spring' for forty-eight years. The carts were not covered, freezing rain beat down non-stop, piercing winds blew, his clothing was inadequate, the ways were so bumpy that he was almost brained by his own baggage, he had not brought enough food and survived on eggs and milk for a fortnight, he could hardly sleep, and he started to cough blood. Just before dawn on 6th May he was thrown from the cart and nearly killed in a collision with three mail troikas. The closer he approached Tomsk, the more the flooding rivers slowed him down. He waited hours for, and risked his life on, flimsy ferries. He felt an 'utter loneliness such as I have never known before'. This leg of the journey took nearly a fortnight and he recuperated in Tomsk for six days.

For the next 1400 miles overland – from Tomsk to Irkutsk – Chekhov bought a large tarantas with a wickerwork roof but no springs ('Siberia doesn't recognise springs'). He had three paying passengers, military men, and they set out from Tomsk on 21st May. The problem now was 'inextricable mud'. The tarantas broke down twice and it took a week to cover the 350 miles to Krasnoiarsk. Here the mighty Enisei river and the mountains beyond it were 'the first original and new thing' Chekhov had seen in Siberia. It was now hot and his nose and mouth were filled with dust and the smoke from forest fires. He reached Irkutsk on 4th June and stayed a week.

The worst travelling conditions were over. He felt 'unusually healthy'. He crossed Lake Baikal and was bowling along at 130 miles a day towards Sretensk. He reached it on 20th June with an hour to catch the first of two steamers that would take him down the Amur another thousand miles nearer to Sakhalin. In Blagoveshchensk on 27th June he was delighted by the skills of a Japanese prostitute. A week later he reached Nikolaevsk on Russia's eastern seaboard. Here he transferred to the 'Baikal', which took him down the coast, through the Tatar Straits, and across to Sakhalin. It anchored off Aleksandrovsk, Sakhalin's administrative centre, on 10th July. Looking ashore, Chekhov saw large fires burning in the taiga. He felt 'uneasy'. Their flames, smoke and sparks reminded him of Hell.

Amongst many other things, Chekhov's three months on Sakhalin are a tribute to his ability to gain people's confidence and work with them. He had no official papers authorizing him to do anything on the island, only a correspondent's card from *New Times* signed by Suvorin and the editor. At first it looked as though he might not be allowed to disembark (in the manuscript of his dissertation/book he wrote, 'so much the better'), as the local administrators claimed not to know he was coming. However, he got himself rowed ashore and within two days had been passed from person to person until he settled at a Dr Perlin's, who fortuitously was a critic of Sakhalin's administration and a useful informant.

On 12th July Chekhov paid an official visit to General Kononovich, the governor of the island. It went well, possibly aided by Kononovich's family connections with Taganrog. He had in fact been ordered by secret telegram from Petersburg not to allow Chekhov access to any 'state' (i.e. political) prisoners. He offered Chekhov every cooperation after the official visit a week later from Baron Korf, Governor-General of Amur Region. Chekhov dined with both high Tsarist administrators. In his book, he introduces them as courteous, intelligent, even liberal. However, in Chekhovian fashion he subverts this impression elsewhere. Kononovich, for instance, told Chekhov that he was against corporal punishment and that it was 'resorted to extremely rarely on Sakhalin', yet a footnote informs us that 'only 300 yards' from the general's apartment people were regularly birched.

Korf made Chekhov give his word of honour that he would not approach 'politicals', permitted him to collect statistics everywhere, and promised access to the administration's own records. Statistics was a new discipline, which Chekhov was enthusiastic about. It would give him an 'objective' path to a deep knowledge of Sakhalin life. He had ten thousand cards printed with thirteen basic questions that he would fill in as he conducted a census of all convicts and exile-settlers. Rising at five, he spent the next two months interviewing the length and breadth of the island with very little assistance. Even hardened re-offenders opened up to him, as he was a great listener and obviously not 'official'.

The whole island was obsessed with repression. Even chickens were tethered by the foot and pigs wore clogs round their necks. One of the commonest public sounds was the clanking of foot irons as convicts marched through the streets. Bad re-offenders were chained to massive wheelbarrows or kept in dark, unsanitary solitary confinement. Some of the prisons and barracks Chekhov inspected were overcrowded, bed-less, foul-smelling and infested with insects. Warder corruption and the *maidan* (gambling den) were ubiquitous and prisoners illicitly amassed fortunes that led to further violence. One of the commonest crimes committed on the island was murder. Culprits might be hanged, but more likely flogged unconscious with a lash. Chekhov forced himself to watch a prisoner being given ninety lashes for murder, but walked out halfway and had nightmares afterwards. No hangings were carried out whilst he was on the island, but even those officials and a priest who had had to witness them were in shock. The most common form of punishment was thirty to a hundred strokes of the birch. If a team of thirty forced labourers, say, had not completed their day's work, they were all birched. Another punishment was being sent to work in the appalling mines. Most of these penalties were handed out with no legal process and even without records being kept.

Hardly a prisoner or exile-settler on the island was healthy or adequately nourished, Chekhov established. Exposure to Sakhalin's notorious climate and unhygienic living conditions meant that 'consumption' was a common killer. Syphilis and scurvy were also widespread and Chekhov met 'quite a few' people who had gone mad. Prisoners received rations, but these were often inedible because of various scams. Exile-settlers found it difficult to grow food on their plots and sometimes starved to death or committed suicide by eating wild aconite. On arrival, women prisoners were encouraged to cohabit with male convicts – which had civilising side-effects – but prostitution was endemic, involving girls from the age of twelve. Often when groups of people started telling Chekhov how they lived, they broke down in tears. He felt particularly for the children who had accompanied their parents or been born here, as the schools were a sham, just as in the hospitals there were no usable scalpels and he 'never once smelt iodine'.

Yet Chekhov found hope here, too. Three out of five of the convicts had tried to escape and the reason for that was their 'innate desire for freedom', their love of 'home' (the heartland, Russia) and their refusal to accept perpetual severance from society. Children were 'often the only thing that still binds the exiled men and women to life, saves them from despair, from ultimate collapse'; the presence of children was a 'moral support'. There were convicts who cared for their bedridden companions selflessly. A convict church wedding contained moments of 'tender emotion and joy'.

Chekhov himself helped when he could: he dispensed his own medicaments, he held surgeries, he helped convicts with money, he gave one convict his jacket as a wedding present, and he took up their causes. On 10th September Chekhov was given a send-off from the northern part of Sakhalin by friends and convicts alike, and sailed to Korsakovsk in the southern half. Here he completed his census: over 8000 cards in all. On 13th October he left on the cruiser 'Petersburg' for Odessa.

The first port of call was Vladivostok. Avoiding Japan, where there was a cholera epidemic, the 'Petersburg' made for Hong Kong. Here he was impressed by the infrastructure and culture that British imperialism brought compared with the Russian variety. Between Hong Kong and Singapore the ship hit a typhoon and Chekhov kept to his cabin with a loaded revolver, as the captain had told him that if they capsized it was better to shoot oneself than drown. Singapore itself he hardly noticed, as he suddenly felt depressed and 'almost wept'.

His stay on Sakhalin had been extremely intense and demanding. Perhaps the stress had just caught up with him. But perhaps he was also missing his family, as he told them he was, and the twenty year old 'sable-browed' Lika Mizinova, whom he had described to some companions in Siberia as his 'fiancée'?

Travels: Europe
1891

Alternatively, Chekhov had been deeply shaken by the proximity of death. In Vladivostok the ship took on board hundreds of demobbed peasant soldiers returning to Russia. Two of them soon died and their bodies were committed to the sea in sailcloth. 'When you watch a dead person being pitched into the water', he wrote to Suvorin, 'and recall that it's over a mile to the bottom, you become terrified and start to think you yourself are going to die and be thrown in the sea.' Cattle too fell sick, were slaughtered, and flung overboard. In the Indian Ocean Chekhov dived from the ship for a swim and only just managed to scramble back before an approaching shark.

These experiences and those of two of his Sakhalin acquaintances inspired the first fictional work that Chekhov had written for publication in eight months. He began 'Gusev' on Sri Lanka, finished it in Moscow on 22nd December 1890, and it appeared in New Times three days later. It confronts the 'void' even more uncompromisingly than 'A Boring Story'. Gusev is a peasant soldier returning home in a ship like the 'Petersburg', sustained by his visions of family and village. He is ignorant, religious and passive. His companion in the ship's sick bay has intellectual pretensions and is sustained by 'protest'. Death snatches them both. But it is the utter indifference of the sea and even the metal ship that seems to rub the senselessness of existence in our faces, and in a masterstroke the story ends with a shark ripping open Gusev's shroud as he sinks through the water. Chekhov's Christmas readers admired a powerful shift in his writing.

Whilst in the tropics, Chekhov's health had been excellent. In the Greek islands he caught a cold, and the ship arrived off Odessa in a blizzard. Installed in new family accommodation, he developed a fever, headaches, coughing and fibrillation. He stayed indoors for nearly a month before his condition stabilised.

The newspapers had announced Chekhov's return, however, and all his friends wanted to visit him – and see the pet mongoose he had brought back from Sri Lanka that was rummaging everywhere. He started to organise them into collecting money for the improvement of Sakhalin's schools. On 5th January 1891 he telegrammed Kononovich that he would be posting him all the teaching programmes needed to make the schools operational, and shipping books to him in April. On 8th January Chekhov arrived in St Petersburg.

It was a mixed and foreboding visit. Everyone wanted Chekhov to visit them and talk about his travels, but within a week he was writing to his sister: 'I'm surrounded by a dense atmosphere of animosity, which I find extremely difficult to define or comprehend. People throw dinners for me and sing me kitschy hymns of praise, but would gladly eat me. Why?' It was surely a disingenuous question: Chekhov's journey to Sakhalin had won widespread admiration and those of his Petersburg literary colleagues who never stirred beyond their 'circles' were intensely jealous. He might be a close friend of Suvorin, but he was still a 'Moscow writer' and the intellectuals of the two capitals were at loggerheads. This may explain why it was said that during his Petersburg stay he went on about 'having' dusky women in Sri Lanka's palm-groves, or was drunk and boasted that he would seduce the young married authoress Lidiia Avilova. What is documentarily clear is that he spent a great deal of time networking with the higher echelons of Petersburg society to collect books for Sakhalin's schools and set up an orphanage there, in both of which he succeeded.

Staying with the Suvorins, Chekhov hoped to make progress with his long story 'The Duel', which he had begun in 1888, but it was impossible. He returned to Moscow and started worrying about writing his Sakhalin dissertation. The truth was, he was still restless from the previous year. At the beginning of March, then, he leapt at Suvorin's suggestion that they undertake a European tour together. On 17th March 1891, with Suvorin and two of his sons, Chekhov left Petersburg by train for Vienna.

Probably more Russians visited western Europe in the last decades of Tsarism than at any time except the present. To some extent freedom to travel was a sop to the middle classes after repressive measures were taken following the assassination of Alexander II. Moreover, 'Slavophilism' – the belief in the superiority of specifically Russian institutions such as autocracy, Orthodoxy and the village commune – was now on the back foot. The days when Tolstoy or Dostoevsky had visited the West and returned 'revolted', were past. Educated Russians knew that western technology and scientific progress were behind many of their own improvements. They admired European liberties. At this time even Suvorin could be described as a 'westerner'. In the Chekhov family the word 'Europe' had always been used positively.

Chekhov's letters home were exclamatory. 'If only you knew how good Vienna is! The streets are wide, elegantly paved, there are masses of boulevards and squares... and the shops – they're not shops, they're vertigo, a dream! Their windows contain millions of ties alone!' He enumerated the sights and said that it was only here that he had 'really understood that architecture is an art'. Every side street had a bookshop. The cabdrivers wore top hats, had exquisite manners, and read newspapers. 'It's a strange feeling, being able to read and say what you like here.' He had not forgotten his school German. 'The women are beautiful and elegant. In fact everything is devilishly elegant.'

On 22nd March the party arrived in Venice, which had an even stronger effect on him. He wrote four long letters to his family in three days. It was 'the most remarkable city I've seen in my life'. It was 'enchanting', 'blue-eyed', 'sparkling', 'full of *joie de vivre*'. He spent the daytime floating along the 'streets' in a gondola, wandering around St Mark's Square, and as for the evening: 'Lord God above! It's so extraordinary, you could die. You're in a gondola... It's warm, still, starlit... and singing and music come from other gondolas. They are singing opera arias. What fabulous voices!' The public presence of music-making and singing brought him close to tears. He admired the tombs of Canova and Titian: 'Here they bury great artists like kings, in churches; here they don't despise art as people do in Russia.'

Unfortunately, it now began to rain and, as he wrote from Florence, 'Italy without the sun is like a face beneath a mask'. He tired of walking around churches and museums. From Rome he wrote that his feet felt like cotton wool and he yearned for cabbage soup and kasha. He told Suvorin that he wanted to get out of the Holy City and 'lie on some green grass'. Instead, they proceeded to Naples and spent nearly four hours ascending Vesuvius knee-deep in ash. 'I stood on the rim of the crater and looked down... Very frightening, yet you feel an urge to dive in, into the very mouth. I now believe in Hell.'

Four days later they were in Nice and the weather was fine. Chekhov went to Monte Carlo with 500 francs and gambled from five o'clock in the evening until ten at night. He started on a winning streak but ended 'without a single franc'. At least, he felt, he was now 'acquainted with the feeling that this game excites' – it was 'fiendishly addictive'. He wrote in his notebook, 'If the Prince of Monaco has a casino, convicts can certainly be allowed to play cards.' Despite the pleasure Monte Carlo gave him, he unerringly identified its problem: 'There is something hanging in the air here which you feel is offending your decency; tainting nature, the moon, the sound of the waves, with vulgarity.' On 17th April he wrote home saying he was leaving next day via the Italian Alps and Berlin for Russia, and wishing them a happy Easter (it was the first he had not spent with them). In fact, the party left next day for Paris.

On 19th April 1891 the streets of Paris were full of demonstrators. Chekhov, sightseeing, was pushed by a policeman. Three days later he watched the French interior minister being called to account in parliament for the massacre of demonstrators at Fourmies, a town in northern France. It was a democratic spectacle unthinkable in Russia and Chekhov found it 'exceedingly interesting'. On 27th April he wrote to his brother Ivan, 'I'm sick of travelling. I want to get down to work.' The same day, the party entrained for Petersburg.

To outsiders, Chekhov's six-week trip seemed less than successful. If he had done it alone, he said, he would have spent 300 roubles, but because Suvorin insisted on travelling like a lord Chekhov ended up owing him 800. Usually Chekhov found Suvorin's incessant talking congenial, but by the time they reached Paris the 'moaning and nagging' had become unbearable. In Venice they had met the young St Petersburg literary couple Dmitrii Merezhkovskii and Zinaida Gippius, who were vocal in their euphoria about the cultural sights. Suvorin, an inveterate gossip, told them in Rome about Chekhov and the 'green grass'. When they returned to Petersburg, they spread the version that Chekhov had been 'unenthusiastic' about the West and impervious to western culture. This further trivialised him in Petersburgian eyes.

In fact Chekhov had written from Venice that it was perfectly understandable that Merezhkovskii, a 'poor downtrodden Russian', should 'go mad' here amongst so much 'beauty, wealth and freedom'. In Venice he himself felt like 'staying for ever', and 'when you stand in a church listening to the organ, you want to become a Catholic'. He even defended Italy against his painter friend Levitan: it was 'the only country in which you are persuaded that art really is king of everything, and that cheers you up'. When Grigorovich wrote about Chekhov 'diverging' from the West and finding Venice and Florence 'boring', Chekhov expostulated to Suvorin:

I should like to know who… has informed the whole universe that I did not like 'abroad'. Good heavens above, I never squeaked a word to that effect to anyone. What was I supposed to do there? Roar with delight? Smash glass for joy? Hug every Frenchman? Do people think I brought no ideas back with me? Well I believe I did.

Middle Career: Melikhovo
1892–5

The day after Chekhov arrived in Moscow he set off with his family and mongoose for a dacha at Aleksin, ninety miles south of Moscow. A fortnight later they all moved to an idyllic rundown estate at Bogimovo, which was to become the setting of 'The House with a Mezzanine' (1896).

Here Chekhov maintained a gruelling routine. He got up at four and wrote until eleven. He would then go mushrooming or fishing until lunch at one. At three he started his second shift, which ended around nine, after which the family had supper, played cards, acted, or 'philosophised' into the small hours. Three days of the week he worked on Sakhalin, three on 'The Duel', and on Sundays he wrote short money-spinners. He also pursued his voluminous correspondence, especially with Suvorin.

'The Duel' was finished in August 1891. Chekhov had latterly referred to it as a 'novel' and considered it, at a hundred pages, too long to publish in *New Times*. But Suvorin was so enthusiastic about the work that he serialised it twice a week for two months. The Petersburg fraternity accused Chekhov of monopolising space in *New Times*, which led him to explode that his work for *New Times* had never brought him anything but 'harm'. A year later, Suvorin issued 'The Duel' as a book. It went through nine editions. In this form it was still subtitled '*Povest'*', meaning a long short story, but its scale and ambition, plus the fact that in it Chekhov realised a bigger group of individual personalities than in any previous narrative work, meant that it was an impressive step towards a modern novel structure.

Returning to Moscow at the beginning of September, Chekhov became obsessive about buying a small estate. He wrote to Suvorin that 'living within four walls' in his flat had cost him his 'health and appetite', and 'if I am a writer, I need to live among the people'. He spent most of November and December 1891 ill with flu whilst his sister inspected properties in Ukraine. In January and February 1892 he 'went to the people' in Nizhnii Novgorod and Voronezh with initiatives to alleviate a famine that killed about a million peasants. On his return, he learned that his brother Mikhail had arranged for him the purchase of a dilapidated estate forty miles south of Moscow, called Melikhovo.

Chekhov's 'Melikhovo period' is the creative centrepiece of his life. He wrote some of his finest and longest stories there, as well as *The Island of Sakhalin* and *The Seagull*. He moved in on 4th March 1892 and enjoyed its security until 1897, finally leaving on 6th July 1899.

As anyone who visits Melikhovo today can testify, the house is a surprisingly small L-shaped bungalow with outhouses. Chekhov described his purchase as '575 acres (of which 432 are woodland), two ponds, a mangy stream, new house, orchard, piano, three horses, cows, tarantas, trotting buggy, carts, sledges, hotbeds, two dogs, starling boxes, etcetera'. The piano was broken. The house may have been technically 'new' but it had no bathroom or lavatory, was minimally heated, bug-infested, and made largely of wood. The dangers of the latter were graphically brought home a month later when their neighbours' house burned down. Moreover, it might be only two hours by train from Moscow to the nearest station, Lopasnia, but it was nearly nine miles from there to the estate on an earth road that would be treacherous during the thaw.

The whole family set about transforming Melikhovo. It was repainted, repapered, refloored, stoves and a water closet were installed, a Russian bathhouse constructed for local use, the ponds near the house enlarged and stocked with fish, and a fire engine acquired that could pump straight from them. At weekends, when she was at Melikhovo, Chekhov's sister Masha developed a large kitchen garden with 800 cabbages alone. Chekhov's father, at sixty-seven, drew on his peasant roots to till, sow, and order workmen about. Chekhov's mother supervised the kitchen in an outhouse and fed everyone wholesomely. Chekhov himself specialised in growing flowers, especially roses, and planted scores of trees. Mikhail helped a great deal as farm manager, for little material reward (shades of *Uncle Vania* here). According to him, Chekhov was often tending his garden before six. The whole family at Melikhovo rose early and were in bed by ten.

Sometimes, however, it was a remarkably precarious existence. In winter they almost ran out of fodder for their animals and even wood for the stoves, and they were dependent on Moscow for many commodities including good meat and drink. Some of these were brought by Masha, others by the almost constant stream of guests who visited Melikhovo. Chekhov's father's diary pedantically recorded their comings and goings. They included relations who might stay a week, unstable female admirers, literary figures from Suvorin downwards, and even 'passing' students. One friend stayed three years.

Chekhov quickly won over the peasants by holding a regular clinic, making home visits, and treating them. He did all this for free. In an average year, he had a thousand patients. In 1892 and 1893 he organised sanitation and quarantine facilities for the expected cholera epidemic, which came very close. He was co-opted into the local health authority, for which he inspected schools and factories. He raised money for, and himself financed and supervised, the building of three schools, numerous roads, and the refurbishment of two churches. He collected and sent thousands of new books to Taganrog library. He became involved in the running of a modern local mental hospital. In 1897 he ran the national census in the Melikhovo area.

Altogether, Melikhovo was not so much a 'country estate' as a venture, a business employing about twenty people full-time. It attempted to be self-sufficient as a small farm, but it was also a medical centre and public bath, a hotel, a supplier of church-singers (Chekhov father and sons), a source of local initiative, culture and employment. There is no doubt that the driving force was Chekhov himself, although his managerial touch was usually light. He handled peasant employees far more successfully than his father, by a combination of humour, compromise, never raising his voice, and his inimitable eye contact and charm. On the other hand, Masha and Mikhail were so in awe of him that they would not even consider marriage without his approval. The leadership and forward-thinking were Chekhov's, but he left most of the day-to-day running to other people whilst he wrote or went about his social duties. When Chekhov was away, the 'firm' was able to survive – just – but personal relations in the family would deteriorate. As Donald Rayfield has written, 'when Anton was in Melikhovo, harmony reigned'.

Harmony was not, however, what marked the commencement of Chekhov's literary life at Melikhovo. His story 'The Grasshopper' came out in January 1892 and by the end of April the early Impressionist painter Levitan and his 'pupil' Kuvshinnikova had decided it was about them. Levitan had been one of Chekhov's closest friends for the last ten years and Kuvshinnikova had run a Moscow salon that Chekhov frequented before he went to Sakhalin. She was married to a hard-working doctor who kept house for her whilst she entertained Moscow's arty set and pursued an affair with Levitan on painting expeditions. Her situation and even her speech were very close to Chekhov's heroine's; but what could Chekhov's motive be? The story can be read as contrasting the measurable achievements and self-sacrifice of a scientist with the vapid cult of artistic 'genius', or even as an attack on infidelity in marriage. Possibly, though, Chekhov was taking cold revenge on Levitan for flirting with Lika Mizinova the previous summer and drawing her into a triangle with the much older Kuvshinnikova. Levitan now contemplated challenging Chekhov to a duel, and Kuvshinnikova's set cut him off.

Also in April 1892, Chekhov finished 'Ward No.6' and personally delivered it to *The Russian Review* in Moscow. The latter's dilatoriness led Chekhov to withdraw it five weeks later and offer it to *Russian Thought*, which gladly accepted it. Thus the most nightmarish story Chekhov had written since Sakhalin, set mainly in a primitive provincial madhouse, was published by the very journal he had sworn before he left for Sakhalin that he would never work for. It was a sensational development: *Russian Thought* was a standard-bearer of Russian 'grey-suited liberalism', detested *New Times*, and vice versa. But Chekhov's experience with 'The Duel' had shown that the serialization of his longer works in newspapers created problems. It was time for him to place these *povest'*-novels in a 'thick journal', and the *Northern Herald* was now moribund. Suvorin's sons denigrated Chekhov's 'ingratitude' towards their father, and one of them even came down to Moscow on an unrelated matter to slap the editor of *Russian Thought*'s face, which put Chekhov in a difficult position. He broke off relations with the sons, but continued to correspond with Suvorin *père*, who still published collections of his stories netting Chekhov over £50,000 a year.

The second work published by *Russian Thought* was 'The Story of a Nobody'. Suvorin had told him it was unpublishable because the main character was a terrorist. Since that word was unprintable, Chekhov had run through eight titles before settling on the present one. The story was topical in 1893, when many former members of the People's Will Party had renounced terrorism, but is rivetingly topical now. Chekhov takes a man with no name who on the instructions of 'the organisation' has introduced himself as a servant into the St Petersburg household of a government minister's son, with a view to assassinating his father. Chekhov deconstructs both the amorality of this milieu and the inhumanity of terrorism. The image of the two-year old child at the end of the story, in whom the former psychopath focuses all his love and care, is unbearably powerful.

In July 1893 Chekhov finished his dissertation on Sakhalin, in twenty-three chapters. In October it began to come out in *Russian Thought* after each set of chapters was vetted by the censorship and the head of prisons. Both of the latter blocked publication of chapters twenty and twenty-one, which deal with the warders and corporal punishment respectively. Chekhov's description of a lashing, and his relation of others' accounts of hangings, were particularly devastating and he had probably left these subjects to the end in order to get the bulk of the work past the censors. He proposed fighting the ban by appealing to the censor's office and even the Senate. This was not done, however, possibly because it could have prejudiced publication as a book, for which different rules applied. *Russian Thought* duly brought out *The Island of Sakhalin* complete in 1895. It certainly achieved its objective of raising public awareness. It possibly influenced some penal reforms in Siberia. Among the intelligentsia it consolidated Chekhov's 'progressive' reputation.

January 1894 saw publication of 'The Black Monk', widely regarded as one of Chekhov's most disturbing and enigmatic stories. It is said to have been inspired by a nightmare Chekhov had at Melikhovo. Although the work is rooted in the mundane – a commercial horticulturist, his daughter-assistant, an academic philosopher – it rapidly becomes surreal. Both the horticulturist and the academic appear to be 'extreme male types'. The first frenetically constructs a regimented empire of flowers and fruit trees, in which humans toil 'like ants', the second is seduced by the black monk hallucination into thinking he is one of humanity's supermen, to whom the future belongs. Both treat people as things and descend into madness. In Russia, 'The Black Monk' has been read as anticipating totalitarianism.

In March 1894 Chekhov gave himself a holiday in the Crimea. He told a professor whom he met there that what he had published in his lifetime was 'probably less than half' of all he had written; that he had 'a whole suitcase full of unpublished man-uscripts – stories that I've begun, defaced, and not finished'. In his hotel room, however, he wrote a story that he came to regard as his most 'finished'. This was 'The Student', first entitled 'Evening'. It is Good Friday and a seminarist is trudging through the Russian countryside depressed by the thought that the weather, poverty and ignorance around him were probably 'the same' at the time of Rurik (Russia's founder), Ivan the Terrible, Peter the Great... He stops to warm himself by a bonfire and remembers Simon Peter's similar action after Christ's arrest. He retells Christ's betrayal to two peasant women tending the fire and they are moved to tears. As he trudges on, he realises that if they were so moved it must be because 'what happened nine-teen centuries ago bears a relation to the present – to both women, and probably to this desolate countryside, to himself, to all people':

> The past, he thought, was linked to the present by an un-broken chain of events, flowing one from the other. And it seemed to him that he had just glimpsed both ends of this chain: when he reached back and touched one end, the other moved too.

The idea that Christ is the beginning of history is, of course, the student's perception, not Chekhov's assertion. In a work pub-lished at Christmas 1894, 'The Head Gardener's Story', a charac-ter produces a paradox about Christ for which there is, however, biographical documentation in Chekhov's life. 'To believe in God isn't difficult', says the gardener, '... you try believing in *man*! That belief is accessible only to the few who understand and feel Christ.' The surprising suggestion here is that, although humanism is superior to deism, Christ the man is the ideal of humanism. In 1890 Chekhov himself had written to Leont´ev that there was 'one' human morality that 'gave us Jesus Christ', not the other way round.

On his return from the Crimea, Chekhov had his fifth shave with death. He had recently had fibrillations again, something 'went' in his chest, and he almost collapsed. Since moving to Melikhovo, he had had flu, digestive problems, a persistent cough, and piles that were so painful he had to take morphine. He gave up cigarettes in 1893 for Havana cigars, and now he gave up smoking altogether. He reckoned that he had 'five to ten years' of life left.

In late summer 1894 he set out on a complicated itinerary that included the Volga, Sumy, Taganrog, Feodosiia, and then, with Suvorin, Vienna, Abbazia on the Adriatic, Milan, Genoa, Nice and Paris. All the time he was working on another 'novel' that turned into the seventeen-chapter-long 'Three Years'. It appeared in *Russian Thought* in early 1895 and was his longest work of fiction since 'The Duel'. It is a miniature *Buddenbrooks*, plotting Laptev's self-liberation from the stifling institution of a Russian family firm, complicated by his attachment to two entirely different women, one of whom he marries. It is intensely 'Muscovite': the most sustained slice of Moscow life that Chekhov ever wrote.

Once Chekhov's 'estate' at Melikhovo was improved and fully functional, the problem for him was to find enough seclusion from family and guests in which to write. His sister supervised the building of a small cottage not far from the house, which could put up three guests and from which she and Anton could dispense medicine. It was here in the autumn of 1895 that Chekhov settled to write *The Seagull*.

The Female Question
1892-5

Despite the fact that Chekhov frequented brothels and in his twenties seems not to have been a very gentle lover ('women are like hens – they enjoy being hit during intercourse'), in 1891 he wrote to Suvorin that 'in women I love above all beauty'.

It was probably this that attracted him to Lika Mizinova. Ten years his junior, she was a dark ash blonde with the 'grey' eyes of Anna Karenina and an enigmatic smile. In the early years of their relationship, she seemed shy, which gave Chekhov endless scope for teasing and banter. When Chekhov returned from Sakhalin, she hoped to become more than a friend but the only thing that increased was Chekhov's facetiousness. He invented lovers for her, signed himself with grotesque names, indulged in epistolary flirting, and claimed they had two children. She attempted to make Chekhov jealous by flirting with Levitan at Aleksin in 1891, and to whisk Chekhov away with her to the Caucasus in 1892. But nothing was more certain to make Chekhov cool towards someone than their disloyal or manipulative behaviour. In June 1892 he wrote to her, 'There is a big crocodile in you, Lika, and basically I am doing the right thing by obeying common sense rather than my heart, which you have bitten.'

The following year, now desperate for greater intimacy with Chekhov, Mizinova flirted with Potapenko, a Ukrainian writer friend of Chekhov's in his second marriage. She visited Melikhovo with Potapenko, wrote to Chekhov that she was in love with Potapenko, but then lost the plot: she became pregnant by him. In early 1894 she joined Potapenko in Paris, ostensibly to train as an opera singer, but saw little of him as his wife, a formidable woman, was already there. Gradually it became clear that Potapenko was abandoning Lika, to Chekhov's indignation. On his second European trip with Suvorin, in October 1894, Chekhov learned of her pregnancy. She begged him to come to see her in Switzerland and Paris, where she was preparing to have the baby, but for various reasons he did not. Perhaps this was as well: in her lodgings she had surrounded herself with photographs of Chekhov and he would have been cast as the father.

Mizinova and Chekhov did love each other. According to one source, he was going to marry her in 1891 but Suvorin dissuaded him. In fact there were multiple obstacles. Chekhov delighted in her frankness (she called him an 'idiot' and a 'bad doctor'), but in his eyes fickleness precluded a permanent relationship. Similarly, the tinge of Bohemian looseness dismayed him: she claimed that he wanted '*Reinheit*' (purity) in a decent woman, not the availability of 'cheese' (her codeword for sex). Above all, he seems to have concluded that she did not want to become independent as a woman, to pursue her own vocation, to 'get herself a life'. In this respect she differed from all the other main women in Chekhov's life between 1890 and 1896.

Ol′ga Kundasova, five years younger than Chekhov, was not beautiful, although she had taste and could be elegant. Chekhov admired her 'freedom and independence', her logical powers, and her readiness to argue with any man, even Suvorin. She worked as an astronomer, then turned to mathematics, supported herself most of the time, travelled widely, and re-invented herself as a psychiatrist. She was the classic Russian left-wing *émancipée* provoking men to defend their prejudices. Chekhov enjoyed her company 'in small doses'. They occasionally slept together, but she claimed he treated her 'roughly'. She craved an affection that he could not give her.

In the winter of 1894/95 Chekhov had an intensely physical fling, mainly in Moscow's Grand Hotel, with the twenty-three year old bisexual Lidiia Iavorskaia, who was even more of a self-made woman. She had shed her first husband and come to Moscow from Kiev to further her theatrical career, which she did by becoming the mistress of Korsh, ruthlessly publicizing herself, and cultivating a flamboyant acting style. She was beautiful, with a fashionably husky voice. She announced in Mizinova's presence that she intended to marry Chekhov. She extracted a 'promise' from him that he would write a one-act play for her benefit night, which she 'decided' would be called *Daydreams*. In October 1894 she described him as 'my friend, my good kind man' and in January 1895 she was 'the woman who loves only you'. From Iavorskaia Chekhov acquired a silk lingerie fetish.

One of the reasons Chekhov spent so much time reading women writers' manuscripts and helping them to place them with publishers was that he believed in furthering their careers just like men. The 'Female Question' had been hotly debated ten years earlier and there is little doubt that he believed in equal opportunity. He had met Elena Shavrova in 1889 when she was fifteen, and instantly recognised her writing talent. It was not accepted by her family and he encouraged it in order to help her break away (they only became lovers in 1896, when she was married). To the attractive Petersburg authoress Lidiia Avilova (who was married with children and never became Chekhov's lover) he stressed the importance of 'combating women's dependent position within the family'.

Considering the society they lived in, Kundasova, Iavorskaia, Shavrova and Avilova were surprisingly modern women. The evidence is that Chekhov sought out self-reliance in heterosexual relationships. Lika Mizinova could not hold down a job. A woman with her own career would give *Chekhov* more of the 'personal freedom' that he demanded at all costs. 'I promise to be a splendid husband,' he wrote to Suvorin in March 1895, 'but find me a wife who, like the moon, would not appear in my sky every day.'

The Seagull
1896

The Seagull was the first full-length play that Chekhov had written
for six years. Clearly both its theme – the spoliation of youth –
and its theatrical innovations were extremely important to him.

Right from the start, however, the play seemed inauspicious.
After completing the first draft, Chekhov wrote to Suvorin
on 21st November 1895, 'It's turned out a long short story... re-
reading it, I can see yet again that I'm definitely no dramatist.'
When Suvorin read the manuscript, his reaction was that everyone would think that Trigorin in the play 'was' Potapenko, the
seducer of Lika Mizinova. In that case, replied Chekhov, 'my play
has failed before it's reached the stage'. In December a reading
was organised by Iavorskaia in the 'blue drawing room' of her
Moscow hotel. The theatre people present met it with incom-
prehension and consternation. She was certainly not going to risk
her career on it.

Potapenko and Mizinova, in fact, were only two of the autobiographical sources for *The Seagull*. In 1887, like Treplev,
Suvorin's son Vladimir had shot himself after writing a play that
his parent had ignored. Arkadina's character was reminiscent of
Potapenko's wife, and her histrionics parodied several actresses
Chekhov knew. There was even a nod to Iavorskaia in the last
line of Act II of *The Seagull* – 'A dream!' – since this is what
she had 'decided' would be the last line of the one-act play
Chekhov would write her (but never did). In 1895 Lidiia Avilova

had anonymously sent a medallion to Chekhov with a page and line numbers engraved on it that referred to the words in his story 'Neighbours', 'If ever you need my life, come and take it.' Chekhov transferred the incident to his play, with an encoded put-down as a reply. The figures of Trigorin, Dorn and Treplev incorporate documented features of Chekhov himself. After she returned to Russia with her baby in the summer of 1895, Mizinova took up with the Chekhovs again, stayed at Melikhovo 'where I am loved', and there is evidence that in spring 1896 her relationship with Chekhov entered its most intimate phase. This is said to have led Chekhov to revise the play before it was submitted to the censor on 15th March 1896.

The Seagull was a very important project for Chekhov in 1896, but by no means the only one. This year is a prime example of what the writer Bunin meant when he said that Chekhov was 'very light on his feet'.

Immediately after a family New Year, Chekhov left for Petersburg, where he dined with writers, patronised actresses, cultivated Potapenko, and generally socialised. On 15th January he was back in Melikhovo for Mikhail's wedding. Nine days later he was in Petersburg again, staying with Suvorin. The pair walked and talked, went to the theatre and a masked ball together, took the train to Moscow on 13th February, stayed in the same Moscow hotel, and visited Tolstoy on 15th February.

Meanwhile, Chekhov was ruminating on the ending of 'The House with a Mezzanine', which had been started probably in spring 1895. In it the narrator, a landscape painter, wanders into a poetic run-down estate inhabited by a well-mannered widow and her two daughters. He argues with the elder daughter about activism and art, and falls in love with the younger one, known as Misius´, who is ambiguously underdeveloped for her age (seventeen or eighteen). The story is famed as the most 'lyrical' Chekhov ever wrote, and reads like the precursor of twentieth-century works such as Alain Resnais's film *L'Année Dernière à Marienbad* (1961). But Chekhov presented the 'remembered' action more as a dream, as something that may never have occurred, and this made the ending problematical. He decided to finish with a disembodied question: 'Misius', where are you?'

Generally, Chekhov's tuberculosis seemed more under control at Melikhovo, possibly because of the direct sunlight and healthier lifestyle. However, at the beginning of April 1896 he spat blood for four days, which seemed particularly ominous given the folk belief that tuberculosis carried off its victims 'with the spring melt-waters'.

On 18th May, during celebrations for the Moscow coronation of Nicholas II, 1389 people were trampled to death at Khodynka Field in the north-west of the city. A week later Chekhov and Suvorin visited the graves at the adjacent cemetery. Both were deeply shaken by the disaster. Popularly, it was construed as the beginning of the end for the Romanovs; but Anton had never felt any affection for them or their system of government.

In June 1896 an ophthalmologist discovered the cause of severe headaches Chekhov had suffered for the past year: his right eye was short-sighted, his left long-sighted, and he had had a cornea infection. Although Chekhov had possessed pince-nez for some years, he had not regularly worn them and had often mislaid them. He now received a specialist prescription and could be seen wearing them for longer. In photographs at this time he is fashionably coiffured, dapper, and usually smiling, but the glow of youth seems gone.

Chekhov's major prose work in 1896 was the ninety-page 'My Life (A Provincial's Story)'. He started writing it in April, when he described it to Potapenko as 'a novel', and it was serialised from October in 'The Cornfield', a popular monthly magazine that paid Chekhov over £10,000 for it. The narrator whose 'Life' this is, is the key character, but the pace, changes of scene, and weighting of the other characters do feel more like a novel than even 'The Duel'. The narrator is from illustrious middle-class stock; his father is a successful, hilariously bad architect. At first the narrator seems just a dropout, then perhaps a Tolstoyan believing in non-resistance to evil. Gradually the reader understands that his determination not to do the 'respectable' bureaucratic jobs foisted upon him to suit his social status, is right: he is best at, and happiest, doing 'lowly' manual work. He joins a team of peasant housepainters who are paid little and treated badly. The story builds up a despairing sense of the hierarchical, repressive, corrupt mindset on which this provincial town depends, culminating in the narrator's tirade to his father:

> One has to befuddle oneself with vodka, cards, gossip-mongering... not to notice the full horror lurking in these houses. Our town has existed for hundreds of years and in all that time it hasn't given our country a single useful person – not one! You have smothered in the womb everything remotely alive or different! It's a town of shopkeepers, publicans, pen-pushers, hypocrites, a useless town that not a soul would miss if it suddenly disappeared from the face of the earth.

The underlying theme, however, is the destruction of the children by their parents, as in *The Seagull*. The young characters of 'My Life' are constantly suppressing tears. On the other hand, as with 'The Story of a Nobody', an unexpectedly positive ending is achieved when the narrator cherishes and cares for the child that his sister leaves him.

Because of its class issue, 'My Life' had a rough ride through the censorship. The same fate befell *The Seagull* in Petersburg, where Potapenko, of all people, was managing its passage. The censor officially rejected the text for performance, but wrote to Chekhov explaining that he merely wanted him to tone down Treplev's and Sorin's 'acceptance of' Arkadina's cohabitation with Trigorin. Chekhov tinkered with this and told Potapenko that if the censor rejected his changes they should give up. The censor was not satisfied, but Potapenko unilaterally made a few extra changes and the play was cleared on 20th August.

By then Chekhov was on his way to Taganrog. From there he travelled to Rostov-on-Don, thence to Kislovodsk in the middle of the Caucasus, where he spent a night on a freezing cold mountain with a boar-hunter, then back to the sun at Novorossiisk on the Black Sea, and on to Feodosiia in the Crimea to stay with Suvorin. Here on 8th September he received a fateful telegram.

For some reason, right from the start Chekhov had wanted *The Seagull* to be premiered in a state ('Imperial') theatre, rather than a commercial ('private') one. His own preference had been the conservative Moscow Malyi! But somehow the play had been sucked into the Petersburg networks and taken up by the Aleksandrinskii Theatre, which had had such a success with *Ivanov* in 1889. Potapenko now telegrammed for Chekhov's permission to give the opening performance of *The Seagull* to the actress Levkeeva as a benefit night on 17th October. She was a highly popular comedienne and it was not clear which part she would take. However, Chekhov must have agreed to this because on 12th September he invited his cousin Georgii to attend. Two days later the Imperial Scripts Committee, the final hurdle to performance, described the play's '"symbolism", or more accurately "Ibsenism"' as 'wholly unnecessary' and denigrated its 'haphazard' construction.

Back in Moscow, Chekhov tried by post to agree the casting with Suvorin and the play's young director, Karpov, but could not keep up with developments on the ground. Levkeeva was persuaded to relinquish the part of Masha, next considered Polina, then dropped out altogether. *The Seagull* would be playing to a house full of Levkeeva's fans who would have to wait over two hours before they saw her star in a farce, *Happy Day*. Meanwhile, the forty-two year old Savina was having doubts about playing Nina. Neither she nor Chekhov attended the readthrough, which produced turmoil. Chekhov appeared, late, at the fourth rehearsal, but no-one noticed him and he went away wondering whether to halt the production. Vera

Kommissarzhevskaia (thirty-two) was now given the part of Nina. On 14th October Chekhov attended another rehearsal and this time his presence galvanised the cast into an inspired performance. Unfortunately, this experience exhausted them all.

These fissile elements and more combined on the evening of 17th October 1896 to produce a theatrical *skandal* of historic awfulness. Levkeeva's audience wanted comedy. The play was subtitled 'A Comedy' but it was immediately clear it was not a *broad* comedy, so they tried to turn it into one. Nina's monologue beginning 'People, lions, eagles and partridges...' brought the house down. 'Nicely whinged!' shouted someone. '*C'est du Maeterlinck!*' contributed another. When there was nothing they could jeer at, they coughed and chattered. The actors were 'thrown'. According to Chekhov's sister, the 'thin applause' at the end of Act I was 'drowned out by hissing, catcalls, and offensive comments about the author and performers'. The mood amongst the Petersburg journalists and writers in the interval buffet was one of supreme Schadenfreude: Chekhov had at last 'written himself out'.

Sitting in the audience, Chekhov concluded during the second act that the play had flopped. He flitted backstage, sat out the rest of the performance with Levkeeva in her dressing room, took his leave of Karpov with 'It's the author that's failed', and walked away from the theatre. He had dinner alone in a restaurant, then wandered around Petersburg while his friends looked for him. At about two in the morning he let himself into his room at Suvorin's and went to bed, covering his head with the blanket. When Suvorin found him, Chekhov informed him expletively through the blanket that he would never write for the stage again. The next day he left Petersburg 'like a rocket'. At Melikhovo he succumbed to a fever and heavy coughing.

Perhaps the most interesting aspect of this traumatic experience was Chekhov's statement that it was 'the author' that had failed. Only the previous month Suvorin had told Leont′ev that Chekhov was a man of 'enormous self-esteem'. Five days after the disaster Chekhov wrote to Suvorin, 'Yes, my pride was wounded.' In December he elaborated, 'It wasn't the play that failed, but me as a person.' It seems he had deeply wrapped his ego in this play, *knew* how good it was, had manipulated all his friends to be there – and disastrously miscalculated. Further corroboration of Suvorin's insight may be Chekhov's protest that he would have found it 'unbearable' to have had his friends 'advising and commiserating' with him if he had remained in Petersburg.

Immediately after Chekhov's departure Suvorin persuaded Karpov to tweak the script to make it more accessible, and to hold further rehearsals. The reviews were almost all poisonous ('a completely absurd play') and Chekhov was made a laughing-stock of the gutter press.

But the second performance was not until 21st October. The theatre then was packed and it was a resounding success. Appreciations poured in to Chekhov. The Petersburg production was taken off around 5th November, but on 12th November another production opened in Kiev, which a reviewer described as 'a huge success'.

In a note to Suvorin on 18th October, Chekhov had told him to halt the printing of his plays from the copies he had brought with him to Petersburg. Chekhov now changed his mind, and mentioned that they included *Uncle Vania*, 'which no-one in the world knows about'. When had Chekhov managed to transform the pastoral tragi-comedy *The Wood Demon* into the quintessential modern tragedy *Uncle Vania*? Was it in the summer of 1896, or the few weeks before *The Seagull*'s premiere? By a mysterious process, in one year Chekhov had become a fully mature dramatist.

Collapse and Convalescence
1897

On 1st January 1897 Chekhov wrote to Elena Shavrova, 'I'm writing and crossing out, writing and crossing out.' He was referring to his sensational new story 'The Peasants'.

It was a masterpiece of 'making strange'. Peasants still comprised the overwhelming majority of the Russian population, but few writers knew the reality of their lives as well as Chekhov from treating and trying to help them. He described the lives of a community of peasants from summer to spring 'objectively', almost anthropologically, and the result was for them to look like aliens, or Swift's Yahoos. Simultaneously, however, he planted in the story a viewpoint outside the narrator's, namely that of a waiter from a Moscow hotel who had returned to his village to die, and his wife and young daughter. The waiter spends most of his time lying on the bed above the stove. Amid squalor, drunkenness, violence and rape, one moonlit night he 'got down from the stove. He took his waiter's frock coat out of the green chest, put it on and, going over to the window, stroked its sleeves, tugged the tails -- and smiled. Then he carefully took it off, hid it in the chest, and lay down again'. As the wife and daughter go back to Moscow, the former relives her experiences with 'the peasants', blames all their troubles on themselves, but concludes, 'They are still *people*, they suffer and weep as *people*, and there is nothing in their terrible lives for which one could not find a cause.'

Aware of how touchy the censorship was about the peasant question, Chekhov cut a chapter in which the peasants discussed religion and the authorities (it has never been found). Whether the superb extra chapters describing the women's fate in Moscow were written by Chekhov at the same time and dropped for some reason, is unknown. He sent the finished story to Gol´tsev, editor of *Russian Thought*, on 17th March 1897, asking him to have the proofs ready for him to read when he came to Moscow.

In the night of 21st March at Melikhovo Chekhov began to cough up blood, but he still set out next morning for Moscow and took up his room at the Grand. That evening, as he dined with Suvorin, blood suddenly spouted out of his mouth from his right lung. Suvorin took him to his hotel, the Slav Bazaar, where his condition stabilised next day. Chekhov returned to the Grand on 24th. The following day he was haemorrhaging again from the throat and was taken to his old teacher Professor Ostroumov's clinic near Novodevichii monastery. Flowers, cold food, wine and letters poured in from well-wishers. Chekhov took precautions to prevent the news reaching his parents. Avilova brought him the proofs of 'The Peasants'. On 28th March Tolstoy visited Chekhov and they talked so long (partly about life after death) that next morning Chekhov was haemorrhaging again. He was not discharged from the clinic until 10th April.

Meanwhile, 'The Peasants' had fallen foul of the censorship. The April issue of *Russian Thought*, with the story, had been cleared by the Moscow censors' committee, printed, and was ready to go out, when a denunciation of parts of the story was received from a higher authority, followed on 3rd April by a telegram from Petersburg instructing the committee to 'remove page 193 of Chekhov' and if Gol´tsev refused, to arrest him. Gol´tsev complied and the offending page was replaced by one from which a vital twenty-seven lines had been cut. The official reason for this was that Chekhov 'paints too gloomy a picture of the condition of our peasants in the countryside at the present time'.

Back in the countryside, Chekhov had to rest. He was nursed by Lika Mizinova (nursing proved to be her true vocation). He gave up his zemstvo duties, fished, and pottered in the garden.

The press response to 'The Peasants' was immense and enthusiastic. Few Russians actually believed that their peasants were mystical repositories of wisdom and virtue as Tolstoy had implied in *War and Peace* and *Anna Karenina*. Tolstoy considered Chekhov's story 'a sin against the Russian people'. Marxists argued with Populists, who questioned the work's veracity. Mikhailovskii damned it with faint praise, since it contained 'no comprehensive conclusions'. Chekhov had really said the last word on Mikhailovskii when he told a student two years earlier, 'Mikhailovskii is an important sociologist and a failed critic; he is constructed in such a way that he cannot understand what creative literature is.' Realising its popularity, Suvorin brought out a separate edition of 'The Peasants' and then one of the story with 'My Life'. They sold very well.

For the first time, Chekhov had been examined by his medical colleagues and the extent of his pulmonary tuberculosis established. Tubercle bacilli may be suddenly activated by stress, so it is quite possible that his collapse was accelerated by the disaster of *The Seagull*. Chekhov was now officially consumptive and the doctors prescribed a change of lifestyle, more food, and a southern climate from September to May. He left Melikhovo for Biarritz on 31st August 1897.

Over the years, especially through Kundasova's tuition, Chekhov had acquired a working knowledge of French. He read Maupassant and Maeterlinck in the original, for instance, and even contemplated translating Maupassant into Russian. In Biarritz he employed the nineteen year old Margot for French practice and other services. When Leikin encountered Chekhov here, he thought he looked 'completely recovered'. On 22nd September the winds off the Atlantic drove Chekhov and his Russian friends to move to Nice on the Côte d'Azur.

Here Chekhov settled in what was to become his French base: the Pension Russe at 9 Rue Gounod. It was run by a Mme Kruglopoleva, it provided Russian food, and there was always Russian company, even if Chekhov sometimes found it tedious. He made a number of male friends in Nice itself, especially Maksim Kovalevskii, a world-class jurist and sociologist. Margot followed Chekhov to Nice as promised, then vanished. Although Chekhov put on some weight in Nice, he started bleeding again in October and it went on for at least three weeks.

He had not completed any fiction for six months. On 9th October, however, he wrote to his sister, 'The weather's bad, so I bought some paper and am sitting down to write a story.' This was 'Home Sweet Home', a work that would later find an intriguing counterpoint in the last story Chekhov ever published, 'The Bride' (1903). It was immediately followed by 'The Pecheneg', which with devastating humour and great understanding portrays an archetypal provincial bore. Both stories drew on the steppe landscape of Chekhov's youth to create what contemporaries called 'nastroenie', 'mood'. By 20th November Chekhov had written a third story, 'On the Cart', based on his knowledge of the hard lives of young women teachers in village schools. All of these works were sent back to Russia and published in the last two months of 1897. Much later, Kovalevskii recounted how at such times, when he was writing, Chekhov would keep to his room, not even coming down for meals, and eventually reappear pale and haggard.

One of Chekhov's pleasures here was a flutter on the roulette at Monte Carlo. Unlike in 1891, he played cautiously and generally left in credit. But as the autumn wore on, he began to feel that he ought to be returning to Melikhovo. His sister was finding its management too much and his father's divisiveness was worse than ever. From afar, Chekhov attempted to impose his will. Remarkably, after one of the peasant maids gave birth by a man who would not marry her, and Chekhov's father insisted she leave the baby at an orphanage, Chekhov had it brought back to the Melikhovo household and paid the maid a maternity allowance until she could resume work. 'All the inhabitants of Melikhovo complain that you're not here', wrote Masha. 'Build up your health, if not for yourself then for others, because many of these others need you.'

Dreyfus and Democracy
1897–9

The last story that Chekhov began at the Pension Russe in 1897 was 'Visiting Friends'. He wrote it much more slowly than the other three. This is not surprising, as it is possibly the subtlest and most precisely observed study in verbal and non-verbal communication that even Chekhov ever achieved. A couple whose estate is about to go under the hammer invite their friend, a successful lawyer, to visit them, with the object of manipulating him into marrying the wife's younger sister and saving the estate. 'Visiting Friends' drew heavily on Chekhov's memories of the Kiselevs at Babkino, which he had not visited for eight years. It even borrows from the Kiselevs' letters to him, which may explain why it is the only story written by Chekhov since 1892 that he excluded from his 'Collected Works'. This, however, enabled him to reuse the material at the end of his life in *The Cherry Orchard*.

Another reason that Chekhov made slow progress with 'Visiting Friends' is that he was becoming increasingly engrossed in the Dreyfus Affair. In 1894 the French Jewish army officer Alfred Dreyfus was convicted by a military tribunal of passing artillery secrets to the Germans. He was publicly humiliated and transported for life to Devil's Island off French Guiana. These events were accompanied by an anti-Semitic campaign in the right-wing French press. However, the fact that Dreyfus had been denied due process at his court-martial inspired his brother to mount a campaign for his retrial. On 18th October 1897 *Le Figaro* published a letter from the vice-president of the French Senate declaring his belief that Dreyfus was innocent. On 4th November Dreyfus' brother named as the true culprit another officer, Esterhazy. By now the 'Affair' was violently polarising French society and attracting world attention.

On 12th November 1897 Chekhov wrote to a friend that he was studying the press reports 'very carefully' and that his initial impression was that there were 'no traitors, but someone's played a bad joke'. This was remarkably perceptive, as it is now thought that Esterhazy fed the Germans disinformation on the instructions of a group of military intelligence officers who were out of control. By 4th December Chekhov was writing to another friend that he was 'spending all day reading the newspapers, studying the Dreyfus affair' and in his opinion Dreyfus was 'not guilty'. The Pension Russe, like everywhere else, was split into Dreyfusards and anti-Dreyfusards, and Chekhov set about converting the latter into the former.

What made Chekhov so unshakably sure of himself? His scientific training had given him formidable powers of analysis and, although no-one possessed any concrete evidence at this stage, he spotted holes in the anti-Dreyfusard argument from the conduct of the trial to the quality of the graphological expertise and the known character of Esterhazy. He smelt a rat. At the same time, his intimate knowledge of Russian society led him to suspect deeply the monarchist, clerical, secret police and anti-Semitic forces ranged against Dreyfus. He was staking his reputation less on evidence than on his intuition.

After 1st January 1898, however, another factor came into play. On that day Zola published his excoriating open letter '*J'accuse*', designed to provoke the French government into prosecuting him for libel and thus opening the Dreyfus Affair to public scrutiny. Chekhov was 'in raptures', he wrote to Suvorin, about Zola's action. 'France is a wonderful country, and its writers are wonderful too.' Even if Dreyfus were guilty, Chekhov believed,

'Zola is still right, because it is the job of writers not to convict people, not to persecute them, but to stand up even for the guilty once they have been condemned and are being punished... it is better for writers to be a Paul than a Saul.' Regardless of the facts of the Dreyfus Affair, Chekhov was fired up about the moral duty of a writer in any society.

True, Chekhov wrote that 'major writers and artists must engage in politics only in so far as they need to defend themselves from it', but in the case of Russia this meant engaging rather a lot. At Melikhovo, Chekhov was under 'unobtrusive secret police surveillance'. On at least three occasions in his life secret police spies were sent to inform on him, even in Nice. His publishers were threatened with imprisonment if they did not obey the censorship. It was a country with little freedom of speech and even freedom of movement was controlled by the 'internal passport'. In Chekhov's lifetime the Tsarist government had emasculated the independence of the judiciary, undermined the zemstvos and self-government, and pursued official anti-Semitism by 'resettling' thousands of Jews, banning them from certain professions, and instigating pogroms. Suvorin's *New Times* had long been anti-Semitic. Chekhov now found himself in direct conflict with the newspaper, Suvorin, and anti-Semitism in Russian life.

Previously, Chekhov had sought to distinguish Suvorin from the views of his newspaper. In January 1898 he joked to him that he, Chekhov, belonged to a Dreyfus 'syndicate' and had 'already been paid a hundred francs by the Jews' to defend Zola. Three weeks later he described *New Times* as 'simply disgusting' and stopped buying it. He wrote Suvorin a long letter analysing the case. This is said to have 'convinced' Suvorin, but the vilification of Dreyfus and Zola in *New Times* grew even worse. The reason for this, Chekhov told Kovalevskii, was Suvorin's 'extreme spinelessness' in restraining his unstable son Aleksei and cronies, who were taking over the newspaper. They 'poured filth' on Zola in one part of *New Times* whilst pirating one of his novels in another. By the end of February Chekhov was saying that he did not want to write to Suvorin or receive his letters (all of the latter, incidentally, were removed on Suvorin's orders from Chekhov's archive after his death and have not been seen since).

Chekhov's relations with Suvorin were never the same again. In 1899 he wrote to his brother Mikhail that he had 'long ceased corresponding with Suvorin (Dreyfus Affair)'. Thereafter, *New Times* journalists attacked almost everything Chekhov wrote.

It has been said that Chekhov's beliefs 'matured' during his 1897–8 stay in France, but this needs qualifying. Even at school Chekhov had been active in preventing a Jewish classmate from being expelled after an anti-Semitic incident. In 1888 he argued with Aleksei Suvorin Jnr about the 'Jewish question', taking the view that the Pale of Settlement should be abolished, Jews 'let into Russia', and treated 'the same as any other Russian citizens'. The experience of democracy in western Europe undoubtedly sharpened Chekhov's appetite for it, but his personal involvement in the zemstvo movement and local government shows that he was already committed. He was pro-freedom, pro-juries, and campaigned with others against corporal punishment. He spent a year between 1896 and 1897 planning with Gol´tsev to bring out a popular liberal newspaper, only to have it blocked by the authorities. Meanwhile, Populists tried to blackball Chekhov from the Writers Union for writing 'The Peasants'.

One subsequent major disagreement with Suvorin and his newspaper deserves extended quotation. In 1899 riots broke out in Petersburg after the police attacked a student demonstration. Suvorin was forbidden by the authorities to discuss the cause of the riots and to public consternation his newspaper column took the authorities' side. Chekhov protested:

> The state has forbidden you to write, it is forbidding you to tell the truth, this is an abuse of power, but you brush off this abuse and talk about the rights and prerogatives of the state – and this the mind can't quite take in. You talk about

the state's right, but you're not looking at it in terms of right. Rights and justice are the same for the state as for any person in law. If the state wrongly takes a piece of land away from me, then I sue it and the court restores my right; shouldn't it be the same when the state hits me with a Cossack's whip, in the case of violence on the part of the state can't I protest that my right has been violated? The concept of the state must be based on specific legal relationships, otherwise it's a bogeyman, a scary empty word.

Before Sakhalin and after, Chekhov read an impressive range of books on the role of law in modern societies. Kovalevskii, at whose villa Chekhov and others discussed topical issues, was the author of a multi-volume study *The Origin of Modern Democracy*. Chekhov definitely did not believe in all-embracing Utopian political ideologies. His approach to politics towards the end of his life appears to have been pragmatic, democratic and based on the rule of law. If there was a problem – the provision of health-care, schools, famine relief – his response was to take a personal initiative and work with others to solve it. 'I believe in individual people,' he wrote to Orlov in 1899, 'I see salvation in individuals scattered here and there all over Russia, whether they are intellectuals or peasants. They are a power, even though there are few of them'.

The full significance of Chekhov's stand in the Dreyfus Affair became clear much later. The Affair fuelled proto-Fascist conspiracy theorists determined to see it as evidence of 'Jewry's' master plan to destroy 'Christendom'. It was probably between 1897 and 1899 that the so-called 'Protocols of the Elders of Zion' were fabricated in France by the Tsarist secret police, with incalculable consequences for Russian and European Jews in the twentieth century. Chekhov made a moral choice not to go with this paranoia and hatred but to assert tolerance and decency.

Late Career: A New Theatre
1898—9

'I'm doing nothing', Chekhov wrote after finishing 'Visiting Friends'. 'I merely sleep, eat and make oblations to the goddess of love. My current Frenchwoman is a dear sweet creature, twenty-two, with an amazing figure, but all this is beginning to pall now and I want to go home.' Actually, as well as following the Dreyfus Affair, Chekhov was busy on behalf of his home town. By the beginning of March 1898 he had bought 319 volumes of French classical writers, dipped into them himself, and sent them off to Taganrog's public library. Arriving in Paris on 14th April, he set about arranging for an imposing statue to be cast of Peter the Great, Taganrog's founder, which was eventually installed there. His activism continued when he returned to Melikhovo on 5th May: he started collecting money to build his third school, he involved himself in local government again, he proposed a museum in Taganrog, he sent them yet more books. He plainly wanted to pack in as much as possible, including writing, before the autumn frosts would drive him south again.

First, however, he had to attend to a portentous letter from Vladimir Nemirovich-Danchenko dated 25th April 1898. Nemirovich was two years older than Chekhov, a successful playwright, yet in 1896 had turned down the Griboedov Prize for one of his plays because he considered *The Seagull* deserved it more. He now wanted to stage *The Seagull* in the first season of an 'artistic theatre' (later the Moscow Arts) which he had founded with Konstantin Stanislavsky (real name Alekseev) in 1897. Chekhov's play, he wrote, 'particularly grabs me, and I am prepared to bet anything that with a competent, extremely conscientious production *free from clichés*, these hidden dramas and tragedies in *each* character will grab an audience too'. All Nemirovich needed was 'your permission'.

Nemirovich and Stanislavsky were far from alone in wanting to establish a new kind of theatre company in Russia in the 1890s and Chekhov was well aware of the various attempts. On the one hand, the subsidised imperial theatres could afford top actors, but these were not amenable to direction or ensemble playing. The commercial theatres, however, were even more dominated by 'stars' like Iavorskaia. Self-indulgent acting was ubiquitous. Numerous cultural figures, including Suvorin, set up 'independent' theatres to stage more 'literary' contemporary work and cultivate a subtler acting style, but they were reliant on the existing pool of actors and producer-managers. Only Nemirovich and Stanislavsky saw that what was needed was hardworking actors unspoilt by mannerisms, with a 'democratic' approach to the company they worked in, and 'directors' who could ensure the artistic integrity of the production, which would above all serve the author. Chekhov thought highly of Nemirovich and had met Stanislavsky in 1895.

Nevertheless, he prevaricated over a reply. Impatient, Nemirovich wrote again, on 12th May. He told Chekhov that *The Seagull* was the only contemporary play he could 'get worked up about as a director', and Chekhov 'the only contemporary writer of great interest to a theatre company with a model repertoire'. Chekhov's reply has been lost, but he certainly refused. Nemirovich remonstrated, Chekhov was conciliatory, and Nemirovich decided he could at least start work on a production.

Within five weeks of arriving back in Melikhovo, Chekhov had written the *povest'* (long short story) 'Ionych' and the *rasskaz* (short story) 'Man in a Case'. Six weeks later, he completed another two stories, 'Gooseberries' and 'About Love'. All of these are among Chekhov's best-known later works. The first three are about men dominated by a particular trait; they therefore partake of Gogolian exaggeration and allegory. Over five short chapters 'Ionych' plots the degeneration of a doctor from a hard-working young man snubbed by the daughter of a riotously phoney 'cultured' family, into a bloated confirmed bachelor consumed by acquisitiveness. The 'man in a case' is a powerful metaphor for the self buried in protective layers. He exemplifies a belief that has bedevilled successive Russian polities, namely that 'everything is forbidden that is not expressly permitted'. His own fear of the authorities and any innovation – such as bicycles – spreads timidity and dullness over a whole town. In 'Gooseberries' a bureaucrat lives by the dream of buying a small old-world estate, exemplified by the gooseberries he will grow there. When he eats them, he feels he has attained the highest happiness, but his brother knows they are 'hard and sour'. His brother rages to himself about the 'satisfied, happy people' that Russian society is full of, when 'behind the scenes' there is brutality, poverty, ignorance, drunkenness, lies, and 'only dumb statistics protest that so and so many have gone mad, so many buckets of vodka been consumed, so many children died from malnutrition'. In a famous image, he proposes that behind the front door of every 'satisfied, happy person' should stand someone with a little hammer to 'remind them constantly by its rapping that unhappy people exist'. The narrators of these two stories articulate thoughts that undoubtedly had a wider resonance at this point in Russian history. 'Ah, freedom, freedom!' exclaims Burkin in 'Man in a Case'. 'Even a hint, even the mere hope that it is possible lends the soul wings, doesn't it?'

'About Love' moves Chekhov's dialogue with this subject on from the portraits of predatory women in his stories of 1895–6 ('His Spouse', 'Ariadna', 'Anna Round the Neck', 'The House with a Mezzanine'). The narrator falls in love with an apparently happily married woman who simultaneously falls in love with him. The stress of not declaring their love and not living together becomes unbearable – there is a clear suggestion that it nervously undermines the woman and brings on consumption. At this point, however, the relationship is ended by the husband's promotion to a different part of Russia. The narrator draws the Lawrentian conclusion that 'when you love, you should be guided in your decisions by something higher and more important than [others'] happiness or unhappiness, than sin or virtue in the conventional sense'. Yet both the narrator and the wife had consciously decided not to destroy the husband's and children's happiness by eloping. The story has been thought to reflect the depth of Chekhov's attachment to Lidiia Avilova, and his decision not to harm her family by pursuing the affair further. But the evidence is thin.

'Man in a Case', 'Gooseberries' and 'About Love' share characters who are also narrators and Chekhov's avowed intention was to continue the 'series'. He did not, however, so they have become known as his 'little trilogy'.

In the summer of 1898 Chekhov stayed mainly in Melikhovo. A bevy of former girl friends attempted to rendezvous with him now that he was back in Russia, and at least half a dozen visited him, but as well as writing in his cottage he wanted to stay close to the *Seagull* project. He met Nemirovich in Moscow in the middle of June and gave his formal consent to the production. On 21st August Nemirovich wrote to him that he had just held his first discussion of *The Seagull* with the company, lasting four hours. This was encouraging: it left an unheard-of four months for rehearsals! Three days later Nemirovich was enthusing to Chekhov about the company's commitment to the play in their first readthroughs: 'Today we have all endlessly fallen in love with you... If our theatre gets going, I'm certain you'll write another play for us.' In yet another letter, he defended to Chekhov his actors' youth and inexperience, which he saw as an advantage, and their exceptional talent.

It was now the beginning of September and Chekhov had started coughing blood. On 9th September he left Melikhovo for the Crimea, Russia's Riviera, but called in to see the company for himself. He attended three rehearsals of the first half of *The Seagull* and was impressed. Nemirovich actually consulted him. The actors questioned him intelligently. On 14th September he attended a rehearsal of A.K. Tolstoy's *Tsar' Fedor Ioannovich*, with which the first season was to open. Irina, the tsar's wife, was played by thirty year old Ol'ga Knipper. 'A breath of genuine art blew from the stage', wrote Chekhov to Suvorin. 'Best of all was Irina. If I had stayed in Moscow, I would have fallen in love with that Irina.'

Chekhov arrived in Yalta on 18th September. His doctors' orders were to stay there as long as he had in Nice the previous year. According to Baedeker, Yalta was 'the most fashionable and most expensive of the Crimean bathing resorts' and during the season had up to 30,000 inhabitants. Nevertheless it suffered from small-town incestuousness and gossip. Chekhov quickly met Chaliapin, Rakhmaninov and the poet Bal'mont and befriended the headmistress of Yalta's girls school, who made him a governor. He took rooms in a villa, but evidently had other plans. A week after arriving, he went to view a Tatar farmstead twenty miles away, then inspected a plot of land on the edge of Yalta.

Suddenly, from a Yalta bookseller, Chekhov learned of the death of his father. He telegrammed his sister:

KINGDOM HEAVEN FATHER ETERNAL PEACE SAD DEEPLY SORRY WRITE DETAILS AM WELL DON'T WORRY LOOK AFTER MOTHER.

In a long letter to Masha next day, he poured out his shock and concern. He was sorry for all of them and 'oppressed' by the 'constant awareness' that they were having to cope without him. To others he said that if he had been in Melikhovo he might have been able to save his father. Obviously, at Melikhovo Chekhov had still found his father a difficult man, but he had been the 'main gearwheel' in the 'Melikhovo machine': at the age of seventy-three he was still managing farm labourers, working on the land, carrying heavy sacks. Chekhov immediately realised Melikhovo was finished as a concern and started to prepare his sister and mother for the move.

Before 27th October, Chekhov bought the plot of land at Autka and on that day Masha arrived in Yalta to see it. It adjoined a Tatar cemetery, but had a superb view of the sea and mountains. Together they planned the layout of a villa. A young architect, Shapovalov, designed an original *palazzo* with many cool white planes. Work began in November and the Tatar contractor nicknamed the house 'Buiurnuz' ('As You Like It').

Chekhov was now settled in the villa of an old acquaintance, Ilovaiskaia, where he swiftly produced another quartet of stories, all published by the end of January 1899. Notebook jottings for these stretched back seven years. The most celebrated is 'Ducksie', also known in English as 'The Darling' and 'Angel'. She is a simple young woman who must always have someone to love – not to 'be in love with', but to *love*. She is empathy in the extreme. She enters so strongly into the 'selves' of her two husbands and a partner – theatre manager, timber merchant and army vet – that in each case she acquires their very language and can imagine no other. Contemporary feminists saw her as a doormat. Another way of looking at her is as a living example of 'kenosis', the Orthodox virtue of 'emptying oneself out' in the love and service of others. The final object of her love is someone else's child. This was Tolstoy's favourite Chekhov story, which he read many times to visitors. The other three stories, however, are also amongst Chekhov's finest treatments of quite distinct subjects. In 'An Incident from Practice', for example, he presents an enthralling case of psychotherapy. Chekhov had now entered his final and greatest phase as a storyteller.

In Moscow, the Arts Theatre's opening season was faltering. *The Seagull* was the last production to open after plays by Hauptmann, Shakespeare, Goldoni and others. On 17th October

1898 it was accorded the supreme mark of theatrical success when the curtain closed at the end of Act I to 'sepulchral silence' (Stanislavsky), which erupted into tumultuous applause. After the third act the company was given a standing ovation. None of the storyline, the 'mood', or the psychological subtleties of the play, Nemirovich wrote to Chekhov, had been lost on the audience. The reviews were 'ecstatic', the rest of the run sold out, and the Moscow Arts had survived its difficult birth. Undoubtedly, much of this was due to Stanislavsky's 'amazing *mise en scène*', as Chekhov put it, 'the like of which has never been seen in Russia before'. Nemirovich ended his letter, 'I am endlessly happy. I embrace you. Will you give us *Uncle Vania?*' For Chekhov, the happiest thing was that he had missed the first night.

In his telegrammed reply, he addressed the whole company: 'Tell everyone I thank them endlessly and with my whole heart. I am sitting in Yalta like Dreyfus on Devil's Island. I yearn to be with you. Your telegram has made me happy and well.' When the Yaltans learned of this, they were miffed. Already the key-note of Chekhov's comments on Yalta was 'tedium'. Nevertheless, he was being drawn more into Yalta society. He published an appeal in its newspaper for donations to help starving children in Samara province and contributed generously himself. He even 'practised slightly' as a doctor, joined the local zemstvo's medical board, and was elected to Yalta's Red Cross committee. His friend Ilovaiskaia, meanwhile, regularly invited Chekhov's young female admirers to meet and entertain him musically. They became known as *antonovki*, 'Anton's Pippins'.

At the very end of 1898 Chekhov was contacted by an old school friend, the *littérateur* Petr Sergeenko, offering to act as his attorney in a proposal from the publisher A.F. Marx to bring out Chekhov's 'Complete Collected Works'. This was something extremely close to Anton's heart. As his yearly output had fallen, he had become largely dependent for income on the sales of his Suvorin-published story collections and performances of his plays. The latter was not negligible: *Uncle Vania* still had not been staged in the capitals, but provincial productions brought him about £11,000 a year, and he was able to divert considerable royalties from *Ivanov* and *The Seagull* to building Melikhovo's school. But a large lump sum could finance his family's permanent establishment in Yalta and the years left to him.

Publishing his collected works had been suggested to Chekhov earlier by Tolstoy, it had been arranged with Suvorin, but the project had then faltered. Marx, a German based in Petersburg, was a tough modern publisher. Parting amicably from Suvorin, by the end of January 1899 Chekhov had sold 'all' his published works to Marx for about £880,000, a third of which was to be paid on signature. Chekhov retained the performance rights to his plays and the income from first publication of new works, which Marx then automatically acquired for a generously rising fee based on length. Chekhov joked that he had become a 'Marxist', and promised not to live beyond eighty.

The day after his attorney Sergeenko signed, Chekhov sent Marx sixty-five stories for the first volume. He then organised a team in Moscow and Petersburg to transcribe all his early work in the ephemeral press and send him the copies. Preparing this edition took up most of Chekhov's working time for the next three years. In 1899 he wrote that all of his 'potency' was being spent on the task. It was, however, an enormous *creative* achievement. To Marx's and many people's horror, the 'Complete Works' shrank to a 'Collected Works' edited to Chekhov's most exacting standards as a mature writer. He rejected hundreds of his early works as irredeemable, but meticulously retuned the language of the rest and in some cases radically rewrote them.

March 1899 was warm in Yalta and Chekhov enjoyed planting trees in what was to be the large garden of his new house. On 12th April he arrived in Moscow. The next day he met Teliakovskii, in charge of Moscow's theatres. Evidently Chekhov still had reservations about Nemirovich and Stanislavsky's company, as in February he had offered *Uncle Vania* to Moscow's

Malyi Theatre. The latter's actors were keen to perform the play, but the Imperial Scripts Committee insisted on serious changes. Amongst other things, in their report read by Chekhov on arrival in Moscow they found it 'rather strange' that Uncle Vania had become 'disillusioned with Professor Serebriakov's academic greatness as a cultural historian' to the extent of 'pursuing him with pistol shots'. By chance, all three of the Committee present were professors of cultural history... Teliakovskii tried to smooth over the differences, but Chekhov claimed that he could not revise an already published play, and gave it to Nemirovich.

On 18th April, Easter Day, Chekhov did something unprecedented: he paid a formal visit to the household of the actress Ol′ga Knipper's widowed mother. Three weeks later he joined his mother and sister at Melikhovo and Ol′ga Knipper stayed with them for three days. On 24th May Chekhov was back in Moscow. He sat in on rehearsals of *Uncle Vania*, which he found 'remarkable'. He now put Melikhovo on the market and started clearing the house.

By arrangement, Chekhov and Knipper met in the Black Sea port of Novorossiisk on 18th July, whence they sailed to Yalta. They took separate lodgings and Knipper was, so Chekhov told his sister, 'down in the dumps'. This may have been because she heard from Yaltans that Chekhov had a 'fiancée', the nineteen year old Nadia Ternovskaia, whom Ilovaiskaia was indeed plotting to marry to him. 'Naden′ka', as he called her, was a 'Pippin' selected by Chekhov to go on excursions with him because she was lively, pretty, a good pianist, and never mentioned literature. However, as Chekhov and Knipper visited the local sights and watched Chekhov's house 'Buiurnuz' taking shape, Knipper's spirits lifted. Evidently, on the fifty-mile carriage ride from Yalta through the mountains to Bakhchisarai something special happened. Five months later Knipper referred in a letter to an 'agreement' that they had made then. They took the train to Moscow together and Chekhov stayed there until 25th August, when bronchitis and haemorrhaging drove him back to Yalta.

It was now possible for Chekhov to move into a part of the house. His mother and sister arrived shortly afterwards. Around this time a revealing incident took place. A village schoolmaster arrived on foot from twenty-five miles away to ask Chekhov's advice on how to save his school, which could not afford its maintenance costs. Chekhov gave him all the ready cash in the house, 500 roubles (about £6000), and took an active part in building a new school. He had already financially supported many TB-sufferers who had come to Yalta to die. He now spearheaded the campaign to build a sanatorium. The first 25,000 roubles from Marx was spent and no more was due until December.

On 26th October 1899 *Uncle Vania* opened in Moscow. The production had an uncertain start, but went from strength to strength. If anything, its impact was more profound than *The Seagull* and the ensemble more equal. It became Chekhov's favourite Moscow Arts interpretation of his plays.

Having fulfilled his contractual obligation to supply within six months a copy of all his published works (more rewriting was done in proof), Chekhov was able in September to start his first new work that year. It was finished by the end of October and published in *Russian Thought* in December. This was 'The Lady with the Little Dog', the 'world's best short story' (Aleksandr Chudakov).

Wooing Ol'ga
1900−2

Chekhov's love for Ol'ga Knipper was the most important event of the last five years of his life. Inevitably, therefore, biographers have speculated on how autobiographical 'The Lady with the Little Dog' is.

Speculations remain speculations, but ascertainable parallels are possibly significant. Chekhov's own experience of women had been as 'numerous' as that of his character Gurov. Each relationship with, for example, Karatygina, Kundasova, Avilova and especially Mizinova, had also turned into 'a huge, extremely complicated problem', a 'burdensome situation' that he had walked away from. On Knipper's visit to Yalta, they had gone to Oreanda and sat on the bench by the church, facing the sea, exactly as in the ethereal scene of the story. When Chekhov had to leave Knipper in Moscow and return to Yalta, her 'presence' haunted him just as Anna von Diederitz's did Gurov:

> I'm hardly in the garden at all, I sit indoors thinking of you. And when I passed Bakhchisarai, I thought of you, and of our trip there. Dear, extraordinary actress, remarkable woman... I have grown accustomed to you and now I mope and simply cannot reconcile myself to the thought that I shan't see you until the spring.

Judging by his published correspondence, Chekhov had never before written to a woman in such direct, 'vulnerable' terms. This was not the first time he had 'fallen in love', but it was the first time he had loved with the full force of the perfective aspect of the Russian verb, as used in the story: 'loved outright, properly, as one should'.

Both the story and his love raise the question of what Chekhov now thought about marriage. He was one of Russia's most eligible bachelors. Friends and public rumour had been marrying him off for two decades. In 1886 Suvorin had seriously offered his youngest daughter (then nine) to Chekhov in marriage, and did so again in 1900. Petersburg circles repeatedly linked his name with various very rich women. *'Tout Moscou'* buzzed that he was going to marry Iavorskaia, and Mikhail Chekhov wrote encouraging him to marry worthy women friends whom Anton 'liked'. In January 1900 even Chekhov's mother seriously considered 'Naden´ka' a match. All these would have been species of marriage of convenience, as Anna's and Gurov's are in the story. But in 1898 Chekhov had unequivocally answered Mikhail, 'I'm only interested in marriage for love... In family life, the lynchpin is love, sexual attraction, being one flesh, everything else is unreliable and boring, however cleverly we might calculate things.' This closely parallels the sense of 'The Lady with the Little Dog'. The tenderness, humour and *'sostradanie'* ('compassion') that Gurov finds in himself for Anna after their first, self-gratifying sex, from which she suffers extreme guilt, ultimately drive Gurov to the electrifying moment in the provincial theatre when he 'understood clearly that for him now there was no human being in the world closer, dearer and more crucial'. Passion, 'being one flesh', becomes the vital expression of that love.

The unresolved ending of 'The Lady with the Little Dog' (its last word is 'beginning') grows, however, from a Chekhovian paradox that is characteristically easy to overlook. We read that 'Anna and he loved each other like very close, kindred people, like husband and wife, like the dearest of friends'. But the only marriages we have seen in the story are completely loveless! This, then, is Chekhov's buried answer to Tolstoy's and others' reaction that the story condoned adultery and was anti-marriage: it was only anti- the 'sanctity' of marriages of convenience and implied a 'new' marriage that would be an exclusive emotional and physical commitment in love.

Given Chekhov's marriage to the 'personal freedom' and solitude that he needed for his particular kind of art, and Ol´ga Knipper's marriage to the Moscow Arts, the question now looming for Chekhov was, would they ever be able to live 'as' husband and wife, or only 'like'?

Meanwhile, in January 1900 the legal Marxist journal *Life* published Chekhov's next work, 'In the Ravine'. The reason for this setting was that Chekhov had become friendly with the young writer Maxim Gorky (real name Peshkov), who was closely involved with the journal. Chekhov certainly knew what Marxism was, but like many people at the time he believed that Marxists approved of bourgeois capitalism. He therefore thought they might not even publish 'In the Ravine', as it deconstructs the impact of factories on rural people and environments. In this his greatest 'povel' (as these expansive *povest´*-novels have come to be known) Chekhov drew on his intimate knowledge of life around Melikhovo, as he had in 'The Peasants'. Gorky and *Life*'s editors were delighted. The picture of economic exploitation and corruption is nauseating. Soon, however, the narrator employs powerful basic words such as 'sin', 'untruth' and 'evil', and it emerges that the peasant protagonists, even the most corrupt, fundamentally evaluate the terrible events of their lives in Christian terms. The abiding impression of the work is one of *zhalost´* (pity), the supreme virtue of Russian Orthodoxy. The night scene in which two peasants comfort Lipa, who is taking her murdered baby back from the hospital, and the closing scene in which the simple Lipa and her mother give their derelict former patriarch a piece of their own food, are unforgettable. 'In the Ravine' rivals Kierkegaard or Dostoevsky in its understanding of purity of heart.

Confirming his recent pattern of writing three or four stories in one intensive burst, Chekhov followed 'In the Ravine' with a very short story, 'At Christmas', for the *Petersburg Newspaper*. He now published no more stories for over two years. He had at least four in mind, and was still editing his 'Collected Works', but his main creative focus was the theatre. It is no exaggeration to say that the second most important relationship of his last years was with 'his' theatre company.

In April 1900 Knipper and the Moscow Arts arrived in the Crimea. Chekhov saw their production of *Uncle Vania* for the first time. 'Buiurnuz', Chekhov's home, became the daily meeting-place for actors, writers and musicians. Chekhov and Knipper made no secret of their closeness. According to Chekhov's sister, it was the happiest time of his life in Yalta. The tour was successful for the company, but it also had another motive: to prove to Chekhov that they were good enough for him to write a new play specially for them. As the directors knew, Chekhov was already mulling over *Three Sisters*, and they hoped to propel him to his desk.

Within a fortnight, Chekhov left for Moscow, where he met Knipper in the Dresden Hotel. But it was still cold, he developed a fever, and soon returned to Yalta. On 23rd June Knipper arrived in Yalta. She stayed with the Chekhovs for six weeks – Masha and Mrs Chekhov were also in residence and a certain amount of late-night creaking down stairs from Chekhov's bedroom took place ('I absolutely adored that', wrote Knipper from Moscow). During her stay, Chekhov worked on his first draft of *Three Sisters*, which he was to bring to Moscow in person. In his letters now he used the intimate 'thou' form, confirming that they were lovers.

From Moscow, Knipper urged him on with the play, which 'after all is practically ready', but he wrote that 'as soon as I sit down to write, someone sticks their mug round the door'. He was referring to the incredible number of people, from those begging favours to sheer nosey parkers, who called on him unannounced and sat in his study for hours. He told Knipper it was 'not within my power' to 'turn people away'. He snatched intensive spells of writing at his cottage by the sea at Gurzuf, but the first draft dragged on into September and then he went down with flu for ten days.

Knipper's nerves began to fray. It had been bad enough having the 'original Seagull' Komissarzhevskaia come to Yalta during her own last visit and court Chekhov (he was actually offering to send her the new play!). Now Knipper doubted his desire to go to Moscow, his commitment to marrying her, even his love. On 27th September Chekhov wrote to her:

> You want and expect some sort of explanation or long discussion – with serious faces and serious consequences; but I don't know what to say to you, other than something I have said 10,000 times before and will probably carry on saying for a long time, namely that I love you, and that's all I can say. If we are not together at the moment, that's not my fault or yours but the fault of the demon that put the bacilli in me and the love of art in you.

Quite possibly Knipper did not yet appreciate the power of the 'bacilli' over Chekhov's life, for he elegantly concealed it. On 23rd October he arrived in Moscow with his draft of *Three Sisters*, threw himself into theatrical life, stayed far longer in the north than usual, and on 11th December left for Nice.

The company were rehearsing Acts I and II from rewrites that Chekhov completed in Moscow. From the Pension Russe he now sent them new versions of Acts III and IV, followed by a series of lesser changes and advice. As Stanislavsky said, these really enlivened each actor's work in rehearsal.

This time Chekhov was not even in Russia for the first night. On 26th January 1901 he set out with Kovalevskii on a tour of Italy. *Three Sisters* opened on 31st January and he received news of its success in Rome on 4th February. The consensus was that this was a 'thoughtful' success: audiences took time to cope with the unprecedented forces unleashed in Chekhov's first mature 'drama', as he subtitled it. The part of Masha was written for Knipper – to draw on her passionate nature, her zest for life, her occasional moodiness – yet she found it extremely difficult to begin with. Eventually, as she triumphed in the part, she wrote to Chekhov that it had helped her understand 'what kind of actress I am' and 'explain myself to myself'.

In the spring of 1901 the marriage question came to a head. Knipper made it clear that she could no longer spend her holidays at 'Buiurnuz' with Masha and Mrs Chekhov as though Anton and she were just good friends. 'How much longer are we going to be secretive?' she asked. She wanted Chekhov to come to Moscow at Easter and for them to marry then. In the event, she went to Yalta, but this only exasperated her: she felt Chekhov was encouraging her to leave early 'to keep up appearances'. Chekhov was hesitating partly because he knew how his marriage would affect his sister's self-image. He arrived in Moscow on 11th May and submitted himself to a consultant's examination. In a long business letter to Masha in Yalta he mentioned this doctor's advice to go on a *koumiss* (fermented mare's milk) cure in the Urals. It would be 'boring' to go on his own. He would get married, he mentioned casually, but he had left his 'documents' in Yalta. Five days later, Chekhov and Knipper wed in a church ceremony with only four other non-clerics present. Friends and relatives had been invited to a reception at the other end of Moscow, at which the bride and groom never appeared. They were on their way to the Urals. Knipper had not packed her silk bra, but made one when she got there.

At the *koumiss* sanatorium, a reply from Chekhov's sister to his business letter caught up with him. She was appalled by the very idea of his getting married. When the news reached her, she felt marginalised, worthless, jealous, even suicidal.

Chekhov put on weight at the sanatorium, but left a month early. He and his wife arrived in Yalta on 8th July and in August he made a will which he addressed to Masha but placed in Knipper's keeping. He left his money, his house and the income from his plays to Masha and his Gurzuf cottage plus 5000 roubles (£65,000) to Knipper.

In the autumn of 1901 Chekhov and Knipper lived together in Moscow. Chekhov took an active part in the Moscow Arts' life, even personally directing a scene in the revival of *Three Sisters*. They were now hoping for a child. But at the end of October Chekhov had to leave for Yalta's milder climate. Knipper was in tears, he told Miroliubov, but 'I am not asking her to give up the theatre'. He defended her independent career even against herself.

Unfortunately, the theatre season that year was so intensive that she could not get to Yalta even at Christmas. Nemirovich wrote to Chekhov that he was 'very frightened' by Knipper's 'incredible pining for you'. They were reunited in February 1902. Five weeks later, during a hectic tour to Petersburg, Knipper had a miscarriage. She was brought back to 'Buiurnuz' on a stretcher. When the couple finally moved to Moscow in June, Knipper developed excruciating salpingitis (inflammation of the Fallopian tubes). She was nursed by Moscow Arts actors and Chekhov, who by the time she recovered was exhausted and coughing blood. On 5th July they went to recuperate at Liubimovka, Stanislavsky's mother's estate in the Moscow countryside.

This was an idyllic stay for the Chekhovs. Knipper recovered physically, Chekhov fished and gathered material for *The Cherry Orchard*, and they 'ate and slept like bishops'. Yet it led straight into the shakiest period of their marriage.

On 14th August Chekhov left for Yalta, where he had to collect a large debt on the sale of Melikhovo, otherwise he could not afford to become a Moscow Arts shareholder.

He was also coughing blood again, which he concealed. In fact, it seems, Knipper was far from recovered psychologically. She wrote an unpreservable letter to Masha accusing her and Mrs Chekhov senior of enticing Chekhov away from her, and she imagined he was not intending to return to Moscow, which he was. She told Chekhov he treated her 'like a stranger', was undemonstrative towards her because he was too self-sufficient, and needed her 'only as an attractive woman'.

He responded, 'But my good, sweet darling, you're my wife, don't you understand that? My love for you knows no end.'

The Basket-Case
1902–4

'The Bishop', Chekhov's finest poetic prose since 'The Steppe', was published in April 1902. He told Knipper that he had been 'carrying the theme in my head for about fifteen years'. Indeed, it has affinities with 'A Boring Story' of 1889: the terminally ill bishop is vexed by the inability of all around him, even his mother, to communicate with him naturally, directly, without regard to his high clerical rank. During the midnight service for Palm Sunday his own mute tears communicated themselves and the whole congregation began to weep. He has an inborn Christian faith ('his family, perhaps, had been members of the priesthood since Russia's conversion to Christianity'), yet he yearns to escape 'abroad' – away from the monastery and Russian subservience. Just before he dies, on Easter Saturday, he sees himself as 'a simple, ordinary man' striding across fields beneath a vast sunlit sky. He was 'as free as a bird now, could go where he liked!'.

Probably only Chekhov's closest friends understood the parallels between the bishop's sunset and Chekhov's. His mother, a highly superstitious woman of intensely traditional Orthodox beliefs, did not read him, but was in grateful awe of his achievements. The stream of 'petitioners' the bishop receives for hours reminds one of Chekhov's predicament in Yalta. He had often assumed the literary persona of a priest, and he read theological publications. Above all, he knew that death was not far off.

He wrote that he had never been so ill as in the winter of 1902. The haemorrhaging from his lungs was not dramatically worse, but flu, bronchitis, pleurisy and incipient emphysema left him exhausted and he was probably also suffering from intestinal TB. He too fantasised about 'escape': to Algiers, Spitsbergen, Africa, Sri Lanka...

When he returned to Yalta on 16th August 1902, however, he was as active as possible. He resigned as an honorary Academician, after Gorky's election to the same honour had been annulled by the Tsar. Only two other Academicians resigned and Chekhov's action was internationally noted. He transmuted his verbose 1886 sketch *Smoking Can Damage Your Health* into a Beckettian monologue. On 14th October he arrived back in Moscow and began to write his last published story, 'The Bride'.

The Moscow Arts' priority was now to extract *The Cherry Orchard* from Chekhov – they could not survive another year without a play from him. He developed pains in his limbs, however, and relentless coughing, and returned to Yalta at the end of November. Pleurisy laid him low again. He finished the second draft of 'The Bride' at the end of February 1903 and began to write his play soon after. By the beginning of April he was saying that he would have to write the play in Moscow, as he was pestered by visitors. He arrived in Moscow on 24th April and concentrated on proofreading ('The Bride' was utterly rewritten in four sets of proofs). He was examined by Ostroumov, his TB consultant of 1897, and amazed to be told that he should spend his winters near Moscow, where the air was drier. The Chekhovs accordingly set off to view various properties in the Moscow region.

Staying near one, Chekhov made a very interesting confession. He said he was 'tormented' by not knowing 'how' to write from now on. Obviously, with *The Cherry Orchard*, 'The Bride' and at least two other stories on the go, he was not suffering from writer's block. Evidence from several sources suggests he was convinced that momentous changes were about to occur in Russian society, even revolution. He wanted changes and felt that he must address the new mood in a new artistic language, but neither in 'The Bride' nor in *The Cherry Orchard* had he yet established his response to revolution or its potential young bearers.

In the end, *The Cherry Orchard* was finished largely thanks to both Chekhovs returning to Yalta on 9th July 1903 and Knipper acting as a 'Cerberus' to keep visitors away until she left on 19th September. He wrote to Stanislavsky's wife that it had 'turned out not a drama, but a comedy, in places a farce even'. On 21st September he wrote to Knipper, 'The last act will be happy, in fact the whole play is happy, light-hearted.' Four days later he told her that 'however boring my play is, it's got something new' and on 26th September he telegrammed that the first draft was finished. Illness and visitors delayed the rewrite and fair copy. 'Darling, it was so difficult writing this play!' he told Knipper. On 14th October he sent it off to her.

Both 'The Bride', published in December 1903, and *The Cherry Orchard*, premiered on Chekhov's name-day, 17th January 1904, could be said to turn on escape, as did 'The Bishop'. Unlike the heroine of 'Home Sweet Home', Nadia, the heroine of 'The Bride', breaks off her engagement and leaves the 'dead' Chekhovian town for an education – not for revolution as some wished. She 'assumed' she was leaving 'forever', the last words tell us. Women, their ability to survive and create a future, had been a focus of Chekhov's writing for the past decade, but Nadia was read as a very hopeful new departure.

The Cherry Orchard, meanwhile, is Chekhov's 'Requiem' and *Tempest*, but neither beauty nor reconciliation triumphs in it. Lopakhin has the orchard felled, but in the loveless Trofimov and the Gorkian ruffian of Act II far more destructive forces await their hour. In the perspective of history, Stanislavsky was right when he wrote to Chekhov that the play was 'not a comedy, not a farce... but a tragedy'. Chekhov makes it bearable by creating laughter from it. As he vouchsafed, the play's last act is 'happy' – because the heroine escapes from Russia.

The man who walked onto the stage between Acts III and IV of the premiere, to thunderous applause, and stood through speeches celebrating the 'twenty-fifth anniversary' of his literary debut, was stooping, emaciated, and kept coughing. The 'iconic' photographs of Chekhov from the 1900s, in pinstriped jacket and immaculate collar, his hair subtly curled and his beard manicured, with 'trademark' pince-nez, were carefully posed, as was considered legitimate even then. An amateur photograph of Chekhov's face taken in 1904 shows it covered with very fine wrinkles, like crow's-feet, which simply enhance the extraordinary humour of the eyes.

On 15th February Chekhov left for Yalta. He appeared to be struggling on as usual. He followed the fortunes of the Russo-Japanese War closely. He and Knipper discussed by post where they would spend the summer, she confirmed that she desperately wanted a baby still, and Chekhov arrived back in Moscow on 3rd May.

Now he was confined to bed with pleurisy and general collapse. He was visited daily by a German doctor who 'ordered' him to go abroad for treatment. This was a very welcome course to Chekhov and Knipper, as they would enjoy a privacy they could never hope for in Russia. On 3rd June they left for Berlin, and by 11th June were ensconced in the Black Forest spa of Badenweiler, where Chekhov was treated by the highly competent Dr Schwörer, 'married to our Moscow Zhivago'.

The fact that Chekhov and Schwörer were 'colleagues' explains some features of Chekhov's death from heart failure in the Hotel Sommer at three in the morning on 2nd July 1904. When Chekhov sat up and said loudly *Ich sterbe* ('I am dying') he was stating a medical fact. Schwörer ordered a bottle of champagne as that was the accepted custom when a colleague had reached the end. Chekhov took the brimming glass, looked at Knipper, smiled, and said, 'I haven't drunk champagne for ages.' Then he drained the glass, lay on his side, and was gone.

The other person present at Chekhov's death was a young Russian student, Leo Rabeneck, whom Knipper had sent to fetch Schwörer. The following night he observed Chekhov's body being removed from the hotel in a linen-basket. It was not quite long enough and the body had to be put in half-sitting. Rabeneck thought for a moment that he could see 'a flicker of amusement on Anton Pavlovich's face'.

Afterlife

Few authors have 'died into' their readers as quickly as Chekhov. When the cork exploded out of the champagne bottle in the silence of their hotel room, Knipper felt the incident was somehow Chekhovian. Approaching the refrigerator wagon in which Chekhov's body arrived in Moscow, Nemirovich smiled to see it had 'For Oysters' written on the side. Other mourners were disconcerted, then amused, to be confronted by a military band playing (a dead general had returned from Manchuria). The adjective 'Chekhovian' has entered our very language to describe this kind of incongruity.

We cannot say that Chekhov is 'best remembered' for this or that work: he changed the way people *saw* things, and he still does. His exploration of how people relate to each other has completely outlived the 'ideas' that his critics attacked him for not 'expressing' in his work – although he certainly addressed these ideas (for example, Utopianism). He is modern in his attempt to look at life with almost scientific lucidity, and in his free experimentation with genre, form and language. His focus on values, including environmental ones, his belief in the individual, his rejection of all authoritarian thinking, his courage and hope, are still relevant in the twenty-first century.

Chekhov's stories were translated into all the Slav languages within a few years of publication and had a profound impact on other Slav storytellers. Translations into the western European languages followed soon after and influenced the prose of writers as different as Rilke and Thomas Mann. In England, Katherine Mansfield read 'The Steppe' and wrote, 'It is simply one of *the* great stories of the world – a kind of Iliad or Odyssey. I think I will learn this journey by heart.' William Gerhardie, one of the most innovative of twentieth century English novelists, was moulded by his early reading of Chekhov in the original. Irish writers, including Beckett, have felt a particular affinity with Chekhov. 'He is the person to whom I owe the most and whom I read the most often', wrote Edna O'Brien.

In Russia, although an official Communist version of Chekhov was imposed, he remained a hugely popular and subversive writer because freedom bursts from his every pore. Pasternak admitted to modelling his own 'Moscow Zhivago' partly on Chekhov and told his son that one of the inspirations of the Easter poems in his novel was stories like 'The Student'. Chekhov's words 'squeezing the slave out of oneself drop by drop' became part of a famous underground song.

Despite a difficult stage history since George Calderon's production of *The Seagull* in Glasgow in 1909, Chekhov's plays have 'affected the British sense of what theatre can be' (John Russell Brown). As Bernard Shaw recognised, writing for the stage could never be the same after Chekhov. Even the BBC television series *The Royle Family* would probably not have been possible without *Uncle Vania* and *Three Sisters*.

English-speakers continue to 'discover' Chekhov. In the last three decades translators, dramatists and actors have opened up the teeming world of his early comic stories. John Cleese hilariously filmed the nudist 'Romance with Double-Bass', and Rowan Atkinson starred in Michael Frayn's programme of early vaudevilles and stories. It was called *The Sneeze*.

Bibliography

Chekhov, M.P., *Vokrug Chekhova: Vstrechi i vpechatleniia* (Moscow, 1981)

Gitovich, N.I., *Letopis' zhizni i tvorchestva A.P. Chekhova* (Moscow, 1955)

Gromov, Mikhail, *Chekhov*, Seriia 'Zhizn' zamechatel'nykh liudei' (Moscow, 1993)

Gromova-Opul'skaia, L.D., and N.I. Gitovich, *Letopis' zhizni i tvorchestva A.P. Chekhova, tom pervyi, 1860–1888* (Moscow, 2000)

Hingley, Ronald, *A New Life of Anton Chekhov* (London, 1976)

Izmailov, A., *Chekhov, 1860–1904: Biograficheskii nabrosok* (Moscow, 1916)

McVay, Gordon, ed., *Chekhov: A Life in Letters* (London, 1994)

Miles, Patrick, ed., *Chekhov on the British Stage* (Cambridge, 1993)

Pitcher, Harvey, *Chekhov's Leading Lady: A Portrait of the Actress Olga Knipper* (London, 1979)

Rayfield, Donald, *Anton Chekhov: A Life* (London, 1997)

Simmons, Ernest J., *Chekhov: A Biography* (London, 1963)

Tverdokhlebov, I.Iu., *Letopis' zhizni i tvorchestva A.P. Chekhova, tom vtoroi, 1889–aprel' 1891* (Moscow, 2004)

Note on the text

The text follows the Library of Congress system for transliterating Russian words. Exceptions are the common English forms of very well-known Russian names such as Tolstoy and Dostoevsky. Dates are according to the Old Style Russian, rather than European, calendar. All sums of money in pounds are given in today's prices.

Biographical note

Patrick Miles writes plays, poems, short stories and essays and is one of the UK's foremost theatre-translators. His first plays and translations were staged by his own theatre company 1974–7, since when he has worked for the Royal National Theatre, Cambridge Theatre Company, the Abbey Theatre, Dublin, and many others. His association with Russia and the work of Anton Chekhov goes back forty years. He has taught Russian translation and literature at Cambridge University, run his own translation agency for twelve years, and now works mainly on his own writing and commissioned literary translations.

SELECTED TITLES FROM HESPERUS PRESS

Brief Lives

Author	Title
Richard Canning	*Brief Lives: Oscar Wilde*
Melissa Valiska Gregory and Melisa Klimaszewski	*Brief Lives: Charles Dickens*

Classics and Modern Voices

Author	Title	Foreword writer
Jane Austen	*Lesley Castle*	Zoë Heller
Mikhail Bulgakov	*The Fatal Eggs*	Doris Lessing
Joseph Conrad	*Heart of Darkness*	A.N. Wilson
Annie Dillard	*The Maytrees*	
Fyodor Dostoevsky	*The Gambler*	Jonathan Franzen
Thomas Hardy	*Wessex Poems*	Tom Paulin
Franz Kafka	*The Trial*	Zadie Smith
Georges Simenon	*Three Crimes*	
Leo Tolstoy	*Hadji Murat*	Colm Tóibín
Virginia Woolf	*The Platform of Time*	